"Finding the Gold is an amazing story of struggle, acceptance and embracing the power of Universal forces to transform the self on the quest to achieve riches."

-Pat Hiban, cofounder of GoBundance, *New York Times* bestselling author of *6 Steps to 7 Figures*

FINDING THE

A Memoir of Spiritual Growth and Wealth Creation
Through Real Estate Investing

CARLA MORENO

ISBN: 978-1-956955-90-3 (ebook)

ISBN: 978-1-956955-91-0 (paperback)

For my mom and dad, who taught me the most valuable lessons in life, and for my wife, my eternal soul. Thank you for providing me ground and stability while giving me wings to fly high. I love you.

CONTENTS

Word from the Author   ix

Prologue   1
1. Change   9
2. Luck   23
3. Vibration   38
4. Energy   48
5. Pleasure and Pain   56
6. Love and Fear   70
7. Homecoming   83
8. Cause and Effect   93
9. Ebb and Flow   107
10. At the Crossroads   119
11. The Craft   127
12. The Vine of the Dead   143
13. The Circle of Five   153
14. The Vortex   170
15. Ego Death   181
16. Darkness and Light   193
17. Rebirth   205
Epilogue   208

Acknowledgments   211
About the Author   213

WORD FROM THE AUTHOR

"You are an alchemist; make gold of that."

—WILLIAM SHAKESPEARE

In my early 30s, I experienced what Carl Jung would call a midlife crisis. In the middle of all kinds of chaos—emotional, financial, spiritual and legal—I felt lost and confused, like part of me had dissolved.

I looked to great thinkers and philosophers of the past to try to find my way forward and realized that what I was going through was not unique. What Jung called a midlife crisis was similar to what Sigmund Freud called ego death, what St. John of the Cross dubbed "the dark night of the soul" (in his famous poem from the 1500s), what shamans described as a "descent to the underworld" and what Dante wrote about as a journey through hell in *The Divine Comedy*. In short, all of these stories described a process of transformation that began with a crisis that felt like death, and all of which were brought on by significant loss. It was the same thing that happened to me, and only by turning to spiritual teachings, in addition to what I knew about psychology and business, could I find a way through it.

As I learned, all the gentlemen I mentioned were not the first ones to talk about the transformation of the personality through a process of spiritual death and rebirth into a greater sense of wholeness. As early as the third century, alchemists such as the quasi-mythical Hermes Trismegistus understood these principles as well.

Originally, alchemy was an ancient mode of chemistry which tried to transform matter into other matter, specifically base metals into gold. Still, early writings on alchemy make much more sense when interpreted in a spiritual sense rather than a material one. In short, the idea of converting lead into gold is an apt metaphor for the transformation of the self to higher levels of consciousness.

To combine this metaphor with Jung's, I went through a midlife crisis that led me through confusion and darkness (a *nigredo* state, in the language of alchemy) and forced me to confront my mistakes and my shadow side. In alchemy, overcoming this shadow can only happen through intense self-reflection, wherein a person can reach a "whitening" state, also called *albedo,* before finally arriving at a "reddening" or *rubedo* state, which signals that gold has been created.

In this book, I tell the story of my life before and after my own biggest transformation, compiling the tools and principles I've learned throughout my journey that allowed me to do so. Still, the journey of self-discovery is never-ending, because we are ever-evolving creatures with ever-evolving shadows waiting to be brought to light.

Throughout my life, I've faced the challenges of family strife, immigrating to a new country, leaving stability for entrepreneurship and trying to find financial independence and fulfillment through real estate. But perhaps above all, this is a memoir about the personal and spiritual journey I had to go through to achieve *any* of those things—and of the spiritual obstacles that anyone who tries to do the same might also encounter.

By telling my story, I hope to help readers identify where they are in their own journeys of transformation, and that the lessons I share are just as relevant to them as they were to me. Although this book does contain information about how to grow wealth, it would be impossible to write without acknowledging the simple spiritual principles beneath all kinds of wealth creation, both material and spiritual: wealth starts with mindset.

When the sun is shining and the birds are chirping, when the pendulum of life is swinging in our favor, it's easy to be grateful—but when we go through crises, the pendulum swings against us and chaos and darkness reign, our view of life can change almost instantly. If we're not careful, we can fall into despair and hopelessness, questioning everything we thought we knew, leaving us to wonder:

Why is this happening to me? Why me? Why now?

In life's darkest moments, it can feel like our identity and sense of self are shattering all at once. It can be hard *not* to break into pieces, *not* to be ungrateful and *not* to hate. Still, even in extreme circumstances, we can look for the beauty in chaos, uncover lessons, grow and transcend our circumstances.

In the ebb and flow of life, the truth is that we choose to rise or fall. I know, because I've experienced it myself and come out the other side.

I hope readers enjoy my story and use it to find their own

beauty in chaos and convert their own lead into gold in every sense of the phrase. The principles, teachers and lessons throughout my life have allowed me and my wife (to whom I also want to give credit) to become multi-millionaires through real estate and to live the life we envisioned. Still, none of it would've been possible without going through a spiritual death and rebirth, and bringing my shadow into the light and becoming a more conscious version of myself. I believe the same is true for anyone out there striving for greater things.

With that, I'll leave you with a quote from Buddha, who summarized it as well as anyone has:

"What you think, you become. What you feel, you attract. What you imagine, you create."

-Carla Moreno, 2023

PROLOGUE

My attorney and I had a deal in place, I thought. *All I had to do was say "yes" for community service and no jail. Community service and no jail...*

The words echoed in my head, as my shoes clicked down the hall and I left the courtroom in despair. The deal was off, and I had 13 days to turn myself in at the Pasco jail, located in the same town where the prosecutor had alleged that I committed crimes six years prior.

It had been an ambush—and now, I was going to jail. Though the idea was petrifying in itself, even worse was the thought of appearing on the local news. I had seen reporters taking vigorous notes during what felt like the most agonizing 40 minutes of my life. *The same reporters who wrote articles about the success of my business just a few years ago*, I thought.

I knew it was only a matter of time before the articles were on the internet, and it made me want to throw up. My freedom, my reputation and my soul were about to be shattered.

The deadline to turn myself in at the courthouse was just two weeks before my 33rd birthday, and I arrived at 5 pm on the dot to surrender with my wife and my mom beside me. The front of the building was all white bricks, but we pulled around to the back, where everything was the blackest of black: the warehouse doors, the dingy alley and the opaque window next to an intercom.

As I stood waiting, I watched two crows pick at a dead rat in the side of the alley that had been there for God knows how long. *Gross,* I thought. With that, the slate gray intercom crackled to life.

"Can I help you?" The guard's voice was tinny through the tiny box. I steeled myself.

"This is Carla Moreno, and I'm here to surrender," I said.

"Coming to get you now," the voice replied. "Five minutes."

I looked into the pained faces beside me in the few free moments I had left. Both my wife and my mom wanted to cry, but instead smiled, trying to hide their pain.

"Everything is going to be okay," my mom said, her voice shaking. I knew she and my wife were trying to stay strong for me and for one another. When the gates finally whirred to life and slid backward on their tracks, the guards gruffly approached to collect my paperwork, check my ID and put me into handcuffs.

I turned to my wife and mom, whose lips were quivering like mine.

"Be strong," my mom said, hugging me close.

"We'll see you soon, baby," said my wife. *I'm not going to cry,* I kept repeating to myself.

"I'll see you both soon," I replied, blocking out my attorney's voice in the back of my head:

It makes me sick to my stomach to even have to say this, Carla, but try not to act too Latina. You are not a citizen, and if they find out you're here and that you've committed a crime of moral turpitude, immigration could drag you out of jail and try to take you to the Tacoma Deportation Center even though you're a permanent resident.

Although local law enforcement wasn't supposed to ask inmates about their immigration status, I knew that many jails —including the one in Pasco—were known for contacting ICE to interrogate inmates who had Hispanic last names. I shook off the negative thoughts as best I could.

"It's only 10 days, Mom," I said finally, forcing a tiny smile. She nodded and smiled, convinced even if I wasn't. My wife and I both knew the risks ahead, but we chose not to add to my mother's dread by explaining it all to her.

As the heavy metal doors closed behind me, the officers walked me down a long hallway to process me for intake, taking my fingerprints and having me pose for a mugshot under unflattering fluorescent lights. One of the female officers handed me a plastic bag, a folded orange jumpsuit, a pair of panties and a pair of socks.

"We do laundry once a week," she said, "so try to keep them clean." After following her into an adjacent room, she told me to strip off my clothes and put them in the plastic bag.

"Before you put your jumpsuit on," she continued, "I need you to squat and cough a couple times as well." I followed her instructions, completely humiliated, and put the orange jumpsuit on.

I want to disappear from this Earth, I thought.

As the guards walked me farther into the jail, we passed a hall where male inmates were held. They were all being kept in one room, and they took turns pressing against the one small window in the room, craning their heads to get a look at me: a piece of fresh meat.

I tried to tune out their whistling and jeering as the officers pointed to a pile of blankets on the floor in the middle of the corridor and told me to grab one. As I did, an older inmate from another cell called out to get my attention, banging on the window.

"Don't turn around!" one of the officers shouted. "Don't pay any attention to them."

More rattled than ever, I tried to tune out the noise as we approached the end of the corridor to turn towards my holding cell, when a man at the end of the row caught my eye. Unlike everyone else there causing chaos, this man was pounding his fists on his cell door like he was fighting for his life.

"Let me out of here!" he screamed, thrashing around to get the guards' attention. He banged his head and fists angrily against the metal as hard as he could, with his sounds getting louder and louder as we approached. Without missing a step, the guards ignored him and turned me around a corner.

"*Please!*" he shouted, now with an edge of despair in his voice. "Let me out of here!" His voice got quieter and quieter, until it was just another wave, crashing into the ocean of noise behind us.

The guards threw me in a drab 6-by-12 intake cell with cinderblock walls, a cement bench and an exposed metal toilet, which also served as a sink and a source of running water. All the cells were the same, except some were accommodating multiple people; fortunately, it looked like I was going to be in an individual one.

"You're staying here for a couple hours until they transfer you," one of the guards said, catching me staring at the all-in-one toilet. "Then we'll take you to the common area with the other female inmates." I nodded, grateful for the clarification.

The cell was no bigger than a small bathroom and I felt claustrophobic, but at least I wouldn't be here long. *I can handle a couple of hours*, I thought. As I sat on the bench, my jumpsuit suddenly felt too tight. *I'm okay*, I thought. *Everything is going to be okay.*

As time passed, I started feeling stiff from the cold and couldn't stop shivering. I moved around the tiny cell as much as I could to stay warm, but as the hours passed, the room felt smaller and colder.

I kept stretching, meditating and trying to force serenity upon myself until the sun went down and the jail got dark. *How many more hours will I be in here for?* I thought. Seeing that nobody was coming, I tried to keep myself warm by curling into the fetal position on the bench. What followed next was an episode of uncontrollable sobbing.

Day followed night, night followed day, and when the hour was no longer grey, I woke up to three loud knocks on my cell door.

"Moreno!" a guard yelled. "Get up for breakfast!" With that, he slid a small window in the cell door open and handed me a paper bag through it before closing it. I scrambled over to the door and opened the bag. Inside was a boiled egg, an apple and a piece of bread.

"What time is it? And how long have I been here for?" I asked him.

"It's five in the morning," the guard replied. "You've been in this cell for 12 hours."

"Do you know how long I have to stay here before they move me with the other inmates?" I asked. *My mom and my wife must be so worried about me,* I thought, feeling anxiety rising in my chest. *I promised I'd call them as soon as they checked me in.*

"No idea," he replied, already walking away. The weight in my chest was getting heavier and heavier as the hours passed slowly. My stomach growled and I wanted to throw up, but I tried to remain calm, remembering my mom's voice: *Everything is going to be okay, Carlita, everything is going to be okay...*

For hours, the hallway was so frightfully quiet that it made me wonder if the guards had already left for the day and forgotten about me. As my panic rose, I had a growing awareness of how badly I needed to use the toilet. As I confronted the situation and sat down to pee, my whole body tensed up from the cold metal and the even-more-cold cell. *Why does it have to be freezing?* I thought. Not knowing what else to do to stop shivering when I was done, I began to do jumping jacks to feel the blood flow through my body, warming me up and reminding me I was still alive.

Up, down.

What's going to happen to me?

Up, down.

It's okay, this will all be over soon.

Up, down.

But how soon?

Up, down.

If immigration takes me, I'm not going home for a long time.

My mind chewed on itself and my body filled with panic, as a guard finally walked by my cell again. This time, I scrambled to the window and banged to get his attention.

"Excuse me, officer," I said, "but can I please make a phone call?"

"What are you in for?" the guard asked.

"For fraud, but—"

"I have to ask my supervisor," the guard interrupted, "but he's not in for a few more hours."

"What time is it?"

"Noon."

"Can I please get a book or a sheet of paper to write on?" My brain was burning and I needed to keep myself distracted.

"No books 'til 72 hours," the guard replied. "And you need to purchase paper through the commissary." My stomach dropped.

"I won't be in this cell for 72 hours, right?" I asked, scared. The guard itched his head.

"I don't know," he said. "There's a chance you might serve your entire sentence in this cell. Covid is messing things up around here." With that, he turned and left. As the fire in my head rose, I breathed in and out as steadily as I could.

If I stay in this cell for another day, I thought, *I won't come out of here the same person. I know I won't.*

Daunted by my own thoughts, my chest seemed to crack open and tears ran down my face. My heart raced and I began to shake, unsure of what was happening to me. My hands and feet were cold, but the rest of my body was numb.

It felt like a cat was scratching the entire inside of my stomach and my chest, causing a strange sensation of adrenaline and shortness of breath. I felt my heart beat in my throat, and with that, a strange blackness in my soul. I felt stupid. I felt betrayed. I felt guilty. I was in so much pain.

Again, I rushed to the front of the cell and banged on the window.

"Someone please let me out of here!" I shouted as loudly as I could. "I just want my phone call!" I banged and banged, with my voice rising as I remembered the man I'd seen when the guards brought me in—but nobody was coming, just like nobody had for him.

"I need to call my wife!" I begged, crying and banging on the window. "Please! I need to let her know that I'm okay! Please! Let me out of here!"

1

CHANGE

"The only constant in life is change."

—*HERACLITUS*

Of all the stories I heard as a girl growing up in Guadalajara, the one I heard the most was how my parents met. As my dad proudly explained, he had never finished high school, but he had street smarts and was a savvy businessman. On top of managing a VW dealership, he also owned ten taxis and a small fleet of semi-trucks that he rented out in Mexico City—but it was through the VW dealership that he met my mom.

"She was the new secretary," my dad would tell me, "and her eyes and smile melted my heart from the moment I saw her. I couldn't stop thinking about her all night, so the very next day, I asked her to go out with me. It was love at first sight."

"I never knew I could feel so much chemistry with some-one," my mom would add. "I felt an electrical current through my body the first time your dad touched my hand and helped me out of the car. And when he went to kiss me after dinner, as I was chewing on the cherry that came with my sangria, it was game over. I was crazy about him!"

Ten years after their first date, my dad decided to leave his business behind and move to Guadalajara with my mom to have a child together: me. Together, the two of them started a new business—a beauty salon, with my mom taking care of clients and my dad running the books—to support our family and let us all spend as much time as possible together.

From what I knew, theirs was a beautiful love story. However, some cracks started to appear in the story over the years.

Upon leaving Mexico City, my dad also brought along my three half-sisters and their mom, so they could still be close together. Initially, my dad had told my mom that he was separated from his first wife, but that he was still living with her to spend time with my sisters. My mom believed the story, particularly because he brought my sisters along on early dates, but it turned out not to be true. He was still married when they met. My parents briefly separated when my dad's first wife called my mom to tell her the truth shortly after they began dating. Six months later, my mom gave him a second chance when my dad promised his marriage was over and it was my mom he was truly in love with.

Since we lived 432 kilometers away from the rest of our extended family in Mexico City, we rarely saw them. All three of my half-sisters, Raquel, Adriana and Sandy, lived in town, but all of them had understandable differences with both my mom and dad, and seldom came around. All three were already adults when I was born, and Raquel and Adriana never lived in our house with us, though they were always loving towards me. Sandy lived in our house briefly when she was in her 20s and I was seven, which was exciting for me, though the excitement wasn't mutual.

I had heard my parents say that I had a maternal half-brother as well, but I had never met him; all I knew was that his dad took him away when he was a kid, and he had disappeared. As a result, most of my childhood was just me and my parents, and I grew up a little like an only child.

Our family was financially comfortable, and my dad took me with him everywhere he went—along with a very organized diaper bag. The three of us spent a lot of time together in our family salon, and I worked my way through the space as I grew up. First, I was in the corner by the cashier's desk, sleeping in my bassinet; later, as a teenager, I was working the cash register after school. Eventually, I was doing hair and make-up, and was even allowed to enter the forbidden room, or what my mom called the preparation room, once I had enough skill and knowledge to help my mom mix the chemicals to dye hair.

My mom was as talented at understanding and mixing colors as she was at reading people and situations, and understanding vibrations. Many clients went to her because only she could achieve the tone they wanted; others went to her because only she could listen to them the way they needed.

"I think my purpose in life is to encourage people," she said matter-of-factly one day, washing soap off of her hands in one of the salon's wash basins. "It's why I encourage you so much, too. What you can achieve is limitless, Carlita. Everything in life starts with a thought—you just have to desire it with all of your soul. Remember, if you can see it in your mind, you can hold it in your hand." Finally, she turned the tap off and wiped her hands dry.

"*Anything* I want?" I asked, intrigued.

"Anything," she replied. "Just know that to obtain something, something of equal value must be given—oh, and never forget to thank the Universe for granting your wish, even if what you asked for hasn't arrived yet!"

As a child, the instructions seemed out of order to me, but they made more and more sense the more my mother explained them.

"Time is just an illusion. That is why you thank God and the Universe even before your wish becomes true in the physical plane," she'd add.

My mom so enjoyed being in a blissful state that she wasn't good at dealing with unhappy clients who disturbed her peace. During those occasions, my dad would step in and take care of things. Though I didn't realize it at the time, between the two of them, I was getting a crash course in Customer Service 101.

The family salon grew until it had 13 full-time employees and was one of the most popular places in town. It was a business where famous singers and important people would come to get their hair colored and their toes done. My mom was even recognized as one of the best hairdressers in town and was invited to perform at Beauty Triad Fairs around the world. To celebrate her accomplishments, my dad and I would always come along.

"We're the three musketeers," my dad would say. "All for one, and one for all."

I always felt the love my parents had for each other. My dad made my mom laugh like no one else, and my mom would often get lost in my dad's eyes. He always told her how beautiful she was, and I rarely saw them fight.

Similarly, I felt how much love my dad had for me as well. Sometimes, he would sing to me in the morning to wake me up for school. Though I hated his morning breakfasts—raw egg yolk on top of freshly squeezed orange juice, sprinkled with sugar—I knew he was making them with the best intentions.

"My mom used to give me this before school when I was

little just like you," he'd say, reminiscing with a grin on his face. Still, for all the warmth my dad had, I could never understand why he had such an unpredictably angry side or how he could hurt me so badly when he loved me so much.

When I was six years old, a client said hi to me and I was too shy to say it back. A moment later, my dad took me back to the back office and hit me—hard.

"It's for your own good," he said, as I tried to stop crying. "I'm just trying to teach you not to ever disregard customers!" When my mom found out, she was furious.

"Don't you *ever* hit her like that again, Carlos!" she yelled furiously. It was one of the first real fights I'd seen my parents have.

"She had to learn, Lina!" he yelled back. He always won the exchange. For one thing, I *did* learn to greet clients with enthusiasm from that day forward; for another, he never completely broke the habit of hitting me when he got angry to teach me things.

Every time my mom found out my dad had hit me when she wasn't around to defend me, I saw the energy leave her body and I felt her impotence. It reminded me of some stories my mom had told me about my grandfather.

On one occasion when she was about 13, my mom's father had hit her eight-year-old younger brother for taking too long in line getting cotton candy at a fair and broke several of his teeth. My mom jumped in to defend him, and my grandpa slapped her so hard that her mouth bled the entire ride back home on the bus. She stopped talking to him after that for only seven months, but she resented him for it for the rest of her life.

Fortunately, my mom felt like she could effectively discipline me with love, even if my dad sometimes felt otherwise. Besides the occasional beating, things were okay—though it frustrated me that my dad would never apologize outright after

13

any of his outbursts. Instead, he would take me out for ice cream and pretend that nothing had ever happened. All the same, I still enjoyed his company. It wasn't until I was about 13 years old that things began to change.

Our family lived in a condo complex, and our downstairs neighbor Rosy had a daughter named Dianna who was a year older than me. She was an only child as well, and as we grew up, we became as close as sisters. One day, I invited her over without permission and she showed up with two guy friends who were about her age. Though I didn't know them personally, I recognized them from school and knew they were trouble.

"You guys can't be here," I told them. "I'll get in trouble with my dad." Before I could stop the two boys, they ran inside anyway and made their way to my parents' bedroom. I ran after them in a panic and saw them grab a pair of walkie-talkies we owned—and before I could stop them, they ran away from me again and left the house with them.

When my dad found out they were missing, I was so afraid that I lied and said that I didn't know what had happened to them. Still, the truth always comes to light eventually, and our cleaning lady later told him that she'd seen what really happened.

"Carla," he shouted from upstairs. "Get up here immediately!" All I could feel was terror as I went up the stairs, watching the cleaning lady coming down and catching her eyes. Both of us were terrified of what was going to happen next. It had been years since my dad had hit me, but I remembered that telltale tone in his voice.

When my mom came home from the salon that night and came up to her room, she was shocked to find me sitting on the floor of my parents' balcony, stiff and staring at a wall with my legs bleeding from wounds caused by a belt. There was enough blood that it was attracting ants that were crawling all over me. The wounds were bad enough that I would have to skip a swimming event I had a few days later to avoid anyone asking questions.

After finding me, she cleaned me up, tucked me into bed, caressed me and held me. She waited until I fell asleep to confront my dad about what he'd done. Though I didn't see the fight that he and my mom had that night, the result was that he didn't hit me anymore.

Things were changing, and the three musketeers were breaking apart. My dad's outbursts at my mom were getting more frequent, especially when he was drinking, and my resentment and disrespect towards him were growing every day. More and more, I felt the need to defend my mom.

"You two are always teaming up against me!" he shouted at us after a fight one day. "And *you* are the apple of discord!" It was something he would yell at me almost every time I sided with my mom. Though he had stopped hitting me, he still used his words to wound—and sometimes they hurt just as much.

In my teen years, my mom didn't laugh as often, and she was constantly getting sick. In the middle of it all, my mom developed endometriosis, a condition that made it painful for her to have intercourse, which, in turn, probably made my dad resent her (and perhaps me).

Fighting in our house became a constant, and to avoid too many confrontations, my mom started keeping her head down and telling my father "yes" to everything he would ask for. She was slowly starting to lose her voice—and seeing what was happening to her, I felt like I had to stand up and find my own, which only made things worse.

The most common fight we would have was over my wardrobe choices. I would dye my hair pink, cut it short and pierce my nose, all while trying out different fashion styles. To my dad, what I wore was always too short, too long, or just too *something*.

"Why are you doing this?" he would ask angrily. "Your older sisters never dressed like you!"

"Dad, I'm 15 years old and I want to dress how I want!" I would yell back. "I'm not my sisters, and I'm in a process of change—let me discover who I am and what I like!" By exploring so many possibilities, I felt more like a spider building a web instead of a fly trapped in it—and since I wasn't hurting anyone, I saw no harm in constantly changing during my journey of self-discovery. It was like Benjamin Franklin said: "When you are finished changing, you are finished." My dad didn't see things the same way, or maybe he was just scared that I was changing too fast.

The next year, when I was 16, things got even worse. I was friends with one of the hair stylist's assistants that worked at the salon, and we started to become good friends. In Guadalajara, as in other places in this world, status mattered a lot—and for that reason, my dad wasn't particularly excited about my friendship with her. He was even less excited when she introduced me to her brother, Alec, who became my first serious boyfriend.

"He's not at your level!" my dad would say. "Why can't you date someone else?"

"His heart is not any different from anybody else's, Dad," I would argue back.

"But we've spent so much money on your education!" he continued. "Private bilingual schools for you to learn English and build yourself a bright future, and instead you're throwing everything away by dating this guy. He doesn't even speak English!" *How does that have anything to do with love?* I thought, frustrated.

Many of the guys I went to school with *did* speak English,

but most of them were a bit too pretentious for my taste. After getting to know Alec, I liked that he was humble and authentic, and I didn't like my dad saying such negative things about him. *What does he even mean?* I thought.

After countless arguments, my dad eventually gave me permission to go out with him, and we dated for the rest of high school—until he broke the news that he and his family were moving to America. As he explained, they were moving to an area called the Tri-Cities, made up of three small towns called Kennewick, Pasco and Richland, in the eastern part of the State of Washington.

"It won't be forever," Alec said before he left, both of us teary-eyed. "I'll save enough money to buy an F-150. Then in a few years, I'll come back for you!" Most people who left for the United States said they would save money and come back, but they rarely did. Something inside me told me that Alec's story wouldn't be any different.

Just as I suspected, he called me a few months later to confirm as much—though he asked if I wanted to move to Washington to be with him instead.

"Why don't you come up here after you graduate high school?" he suggested. "I'm sure I could get you a job as a hostess at the Mexican restaurant I work at."

The idea of leaving everything behind to move to another country and be with my boyfriend seemed wild. However, it just happened that one of the most famous and prestigious make-up schools, Blanche McDonald, was located in Canada, just 369 miles away from where Alec lived. The idea of applying there as a student to learn professional fashion make-up skills and be closer to Alec at the same time seemed like a plausible plan. Still, since the fights with my dad were only getting worse, I started seriously considering the idea. All I wanted was to be free, and with six months before graduation to think things through, I could craft a plan and save the money I needed to make it happen.

Unfortunately, my dad caught wind of my plan earlier than I had expected.

"I don't understand why you're still dating that boy," my dad grumbled.

"Dad," I began, finding my courage, "I'm not asking you for money. I'm an adult now, and I've saved for my own expenses. And as an adult, I'm not asking you, I'm telling you that I'm going to Washington." We went around and around for a little while longer, but my dad soon realized that there was nothing he could hold over me. There was nothing that would stop me from doing what I had planned to do.

"You're not going," he said gruffly. "I am your father, and you have to do as I say!"

"I'm leaving, Dad," I told him.

"We'll see," he replied.

One Sunday morning soon after, I was walking our dog and came back into the kitchen where I caught my dad sitting at the table. He looked like he'd been up all night about something and now couldn't wait to tell me what it was.

"I'm not letting you go, Carla," he said, catching me entirely off guard. I blinked at him once and then kept doing what I was doing, trying not to engage. "Did you hear me?" he asked, the anger rising in his voice.

"You can't stop me," I said simply.

"Don't make me do anything I'll regret," my dad growled. His fist was clenched and he was practically vibrating with rage.

"I'm not a kid anymore!" I screamed, loud enough to surprise him (and myself). "You can't just hit me, or I'll call the police. Try to hit me, I dare you!" Up until that day, my dad's tensed jaw and the gaze in his eye had usually frozen me with terror—but now, something more powerful inside me took over. This time, I stayed in my body.

Soon we were both swinging wildly at one another and my mom rushed in to defend me and break us up. All three of us were tangled together and rolling up against the dining room table and chairs, like tumbleweeds in a tornado. I wasn't sure how it happened but when we finally separated, we were 15 feet away from where the confrontation began.

Fuck, I thought. *What just happened?* Confused, I wiped my face with the back of my hand and drew it back with blood on it. Then I saw a look in my dad's eyes—and again, the fear came rushing back worse than it had before.

I ran into the bedroom to call 911, but my dad rushed in behind me and violently pulled the cable lines out of the wall. I bolted past him into the hall, but he kept chasing me. *I have to get out of this house,* I thought over and over, my entire body shaking.

I kept running until I was at the door of my downstairs neighbor, Rosy, and knocked loudly until she opened it and gasped.

"What happened to you?" she asked, pulling me inside.

"Can I use your phone?" I asked, ignoring her question. "I need to call the police to calm my dad down." With that, Rosy rushed to bring me a phone and I called 911, fearing for my mom's safety. After the longest 10 minutes of my life, two police officers came to Rosy's door and escorted me back upstairs.

To my surprise, my dad was calm and poised now that the officers were around. He invited them inside and we all sat on the couch to explain our different versions of what happened, with the police taking notes the whole time. At the end of it all, my dad shrugged.

"One simply cannot let the birds shoot at guns," he said

offhandedly. It was a Mexican idiom he loved to say, and he meant it to sound smooth and authoritative—but it must have come out cocky and unpleasant because the officers suddenly frowned, stood up and pulled their handcuffs out.

"You're gonna have to come with us, sir," one of the officers said. After a struggle, the officers had him in handcuffs.

"Why are you taking him?" I asked. I was suddenly questioning what I'd actually intended when I called the police. "I just wanted you to calm him down. That's all!"

"I'm sorry, but we have to take him," another officer replied. "It's not up to you anymore. It'll only be eight hours, which should give him enough time to calm down."

After eight hours in jail, my dad came back home—but calm he was not. If anything, he was 10 times angrier than he had been before. We heard him talking to Sandy and venting about the situation.

"They're going to regret this," my dad said, with the phone on speaker for all to hear.

For the next few days, my mom and I barely left my bedroom. We snuck around the house, using the closest bathroom and grabbing food from the kitchen whenever I thought my dad wasn't around. While we kept avoiding him, we could still hear his anger as he stomped around, or when he was banging cabinets or slamming doors.

"Mom, I can't do this anymore," I said quietly. "I have to go to America." I was scared for my mom, but I knew she could handle my dad better than I could. He had also never been physically aggressive towards her (until that day, at least).

"I understand, Carlita," my mom said. "It will hurt my soul for you to leave, but I know you have to. You have my full support."

For the next couple of weeks, my mom and I both avoided

my dad and made a plan to ensure my safe escape. First, we called Alec's family and explained the situation to them.

"We're going to send Carla to the United States for a few months until she's able to apply to school and move to Canada," my mom said carefully, "and it would be wonderful if you could keep an eye on her."

After a few phone calls, it was settled that I would stay with Alec's family in Pasco, and despite all the chaos, he and I were excited to be reunited. Finally, on the day of my flight, my father and I crossed paths in the kitchen. I had my bags packed and my mom was in the car outside, ready to take me to the airport.

"You're leaving today?" My dad asked quietly. I nodded, my hand balling up instinctively. I expected him to be angry again, but instead I just felt the sadness in his soul. He nodded also, breaking eye contact.

"I don't want you to leave on bad terms," he said, understanding there was nothing he could do at that point to make me change my mind. Outside, I heard my mom's voice.

"Carla, let's go! We're going to be late!" she shouted.

"I've got to go, Dad," I said, my voice shaking a little. He nodded again.

"Well, be careful," he said. With that, he walked over to hug me. "Goodbye, Carla."

After our hug, I marched out the door, threw my bag in the backseat of the car and got in the front. As I pulled on my seatbelt and my mom started the engine, I saw my dad standing in the window, watching us pull out of the driveway.

Our drive to Guadalajara International Airport was quiet until we pulled up to my terminal. Then we both started crying.

"Goodbye, mi chiquita," my mom said, trying to smile. She pulled out a small wad of bills and pressed them into my hand.

"I tried to get as much money for you as I could, but you know how your father is."

"Thanks, Mom," I smiled back. After we said our goodbyes, I checked my bags, printed my boarding pass and made my way through the airport. They announced the flight to Pasco and I boarded the plane, took my seat by the window and burst into tears.

Was I really leaving my mom behind? Couldn't she come with me? Of course, I knew she couldn't—she had her business in Mexico, and all of her assets were under my dad's name, including her savings. He had always told her that if they ever needed to divorce, he would give her half. She had trusted him, but now I suspected she shouldn't have.

After the flight attendant announced the safety procedures, I watched out the window as the plane took off and Guadalajara got smaller and smaller behind me. When we broke through the clouds, I took out the bills and counted $500.

As the plane rose, I did my best to ignore the knot in my stomach. *I'm going to America*, I thought.

2

LUCK

"Luck is what happens when preparation meets opportunity."

—SENECA

After seven hours in the air, the plane's wheels touched the runway at Tri-Cities Airport in Pasco, where Alec and my new life were waiting for me.

My dad had always wanted me to move to America and make something of myself; it was part of why my parents had spent so much on private schools and teaching me English when I was young.

"I want you to be prepared so that one day you can fulfill the dream I could never materialize," he told me once, "to live in America." He always thought it was harder to have great business success in Mexico, particularly because of political corruption and other kinds of local insecurity.

When I had visited America before, I'd imagined how my life would be different in a new place. This time was different. This time, even though I didn't have his support and couldn't go home, I felt a responsibility to fulfill my dad's dream—but on my terms, not his. Even if Alec and his family could offer me some support, it was still up to me to take care of myself.

In the quiet moments while Alec and I waited for my luggage, my dad's words kept coming back:

We spent so much money on your education for you to throw away your future with that boyfriend of yours!

I had to prove him wrong.

Now that I was in the land of opportunity, I was determined to use the tools that both of my parents had taught me. My dad had taught me how to be resilient in my body, and my mom had strengthened my mind and helped me believe in myself. Now, it was up to me to find my own way and add my soul to the equation.

"What you think about is what will become real, Carlita," my mom had told me. "You have to be careful what you focus on and how you think, because your thoughts create your reality." She understood the power of the law of attraction, and I had to use it as well. *I have to focus on making it*, I thought. *I have to find out what I'm capable of.*

The next day, once I had settled in and unpacked a little, I put together the most alluring look I could and had Alec drive me to the only mall in the Tri-Cities, the Columbia Mall in Kennewick, where I knew there was a MAC Cosmetics store.

When I got there, I confidently introduced myself to the cashier at the front of the store and she handed me an application, which I promptly filled out in the food court and returned. I had brought all the paperwork I thought I needed with me and asked the cashier as confidently as I could if we could do a quick interview on the spot. She smiled.

"I love your enthusiasm," the young woman said, scanning my application. I beamed.

"It looks like you forgot to fill something out, though," she said, putting the paper down, twisting it around and pushing it towards me. She tapped an empty line twice with a black, manicured fingernail. "Darling, do you have a social security number you can add so we can put you in our system?" I felt the blood drain from my hands. *Oh no.*

"Well," I stammered, turning the application towards her again and pointing at certain lines. "I don't have one yet, but I have a lot of experience. I've been doing makeup at my mom's salon since I was 15. I know I could be a great addition to your team."

"I'm sorry, sweetheart," she replied with an uncomfortable smile, "we need that number, so just come back when you have it with you, okay?" She excused herself to help other customers, who I could tell had overheard the whole thing.

My cheeks burned the whole ride home. I was more than qualified to work a makeup counter! I was a makeup *artist,* and I understood customer service—but I didn't have that nine-digit number.

"I didn't want to crush your dream," Alec said slowly, "but most places will ask you for that number. The good news is: I spoke to my manager, and we can still get you a job at the restaurant. Plus this way, we can ride to work together and avoid a few headaches."

There was only one car for Alec's entire household of five, which now included myself. Both his mom and sister worked at the same nursing home, and Alec and his dad worked at the same restaurant. *It's true,* I thought, *working with Alec at the restaurant is probably the best thing to do...for now.*

At home that night, I turned off the lights to go to sleep. As I listened to the quiet sounds of cars in the twilight, I felt tears forming in my eyes and angrily wiped them away. I missed my mom, my home and my friends.

One or two sharp sobs escaped my mouth before I rolled over into my pillow, remembering where I was. *Get a hold of yourself,* I thought, taking a breath and willing myself to be calm. *You're going to wake someone up.*

The next day, Alec took me to Torito's, a Mexican chain restaurant where he and his dad worked as bussers, to introduce me to the restaurant owner for an interview. Alec pushed the door open with a jingle, revealing an inside that was unremarkable: booths covered with rainbow-colored zarapes, huge sombreros hanging on the walls, towers of Styrofoam takeout containers stacked behind the cash register and a faded mural of the Aztec calendar on one of the walls.

"Meet Carla," Alec said as the owner and I shook hands. "She's ready to work!"

Though it wasn't the job I had in mind, I needed the money and was grateful to have a job where not having a social security number wasn't a problem. I told myself to remain humble and obey orders, even if it meant doing things outside of my job description, like occasionally cleaning the bathrooms. I made myself available to cover extra shifts, even if it sometimes meant working 12 hours a day—especially since it was the best way to get the morning shifts, which were the best ones. No matter what happened, I wanted to stay on the owner's good side. *After all,* I thought, *I'm not the owner's daughter anymore.*

When I touched down in the United States, I had fixated on how unlucky it was that I didn't have a social security number for a while. Still, working at Torito's was changing my mind about luck. In reality, there was no such thing as just "luck." It was really a combination of being in the right place at the right time and being prepared to welcome new opportunities—and I realized that a good portion of that was under my control.

One opportunity came six months later, after my friend Bella, another waitress at Torito's, introduced me to her best friend.

"Carla, this is my friend Lucio," Bella said effusively one day, "the one I was telling you about!" Lucio shook my hand before I showed him to his table. After her shift was over, Bella joined Lucio at his table before inviting Alec and I over once we were clocked out as well. We ordered some margaritas (though I was barely 18, knowing the bartenders meant I could get away with sneaking a drink once in a while) and I decided that I liked Lucio right away. He liked to be the center of attention, but he had a fun personality. He kept making jokes and cracking us up.

In the middle of all our excitement, the subject of me being bilingual came up.

"Do you speak English well?" Lucio asked me.

"Yes, I do," I replied.

"You should become an interpreter," he said brightly. "I'm starting my own company in Seattle, and I could hire you if you pass the test. Girl, you could be making $25 an hour—triple what they're paying you here!"

"Are you serious?" I asked, bemused. Bella was perking up hearing our conversation as well. "How do you do that?"

"It's easy," he replied, waving his hand. "All you have to do is study for the test and get your interpreting license." As Lucio explained, the Tri-Cities were full of Spanish-speaking people, and the area was something like 33 percent Latino. There were lots of migrant farm workers and laborers in the area—people who worked physically demanding jobs and tended to sustain a lot of injuries.

"In Washington, we have no-fault workers' compensation

for most of those industries," Lucio continued. As he explained, every time one of those Spanish-speaking workers got injured or had any kind of health issue (which was often), they had to go through a series of state systems and ended up in local hospitals or health clinics.

"Most doctors around here only speak English," Lucio said finally, "so the hospitals and clinics have to hire interpreters to sit in all those appointments to make sure everyone understands each other."

What he was saying made sense: there were big local companies that hired interpreters as subcontractors and sent them to all kinds of jobs around the Tri-Cities, and they would hire basically anybody who passed the tests.

"Assuming I pass the test," I explained to Lucio, "the problem is I don't have a social security number. Is that going to be a problem?"

"Actually, no," he replied. "You can get a tax ID number and use that instead of a social, because you'd be working as a self-employed contractor. Bella, you should get certified too. I'll hire you both!" Now, we were all getting excited.

"Would we have to move to Seattle?" I asked.

"Not really," Lucio replied. "I'm starting my company there, but my plan is to expand to the Tri-Cities. By the time you both pass your exam, I'm hoping to have appointments available in whatever location you choose." Clearly, Lucio seemed to be a man with big dreams—and meeting him was the exact lucky break I needed to put my bilingual skills to good use.

After meeting Lucio that night, the two of us became fast friends, seeing each other almost every weekend to get drinks along with Bella, Alec and Lucio's soon-to-be wife. Taking his advice, I started preparing for the state's medical interpreter exam right away whenever I wasn't working at Torito's (though sometimes, if the restaurant wasn't busy, I would bring my prep books with me and read them secretly behind my podium or on break).

After two months of studying, Alec drove me to an appointment in Yakima to take the written portion of the test, and in short order, I got the good news: I had passed the written exam! It meant that the state would issue me a provisional certification allowing me to cover certain appointments until I could pass the oral exam and become fully certified. A couple of months later, I passed the oral exam and was officially certified as a medical interpreter.

Lucio had already left for Seattle, but now that I had my newly minted interpreter's license, I wanted to call him right away to give him the good news that I was ready to work.

"Girl, my agency hasn't picked up yet," he said.

"Oh," I said, disappointed.

"Don't worry," he replied, "I'll be in touch soon!" As it turned out, the business never picked up in Seattle, and he was only gone for a few months before he had to return to the Tri-Cities. As he explained, things hadn't worked out for many reasons: there wasn't enough business, there was too much paperwork involved, living in the city was expensive, his business partner was often busy since she was still in school and the party scene was way too tempting.

"I do have some good news though," he said. "I'm working with another agency as a freelancer for the time being, and I can give you their contact so you can work with them, too."

After our conversation, I called the owner of the agency Lucio had recommended and introduced myself, explaining that I was busy in the mornings with shifts at the restaurant but could make myself available between 4pm and 8am. A few hours later, he called me back to say that I'd gotten myself a job.

As the owner explained, the interpreting agency was

contracted with all the local hospitals in the Tri-Cities and covered appointments for the state as well—both by accepting workers' compensation or payments from the Labor and Industries department (also known as L&I) or state insurance, such as people with medical coupons.

After a few days of covering appointments at local clinics, I walked into one of the big hospitals for the first time, not knowing what type of assignment I was showing up for.

"You're our interpreter?" the nurse asked abruptly. I confirmed that I was. "Good," she said, throwing some hospital scrubs at me along with a mask. "We need you in DR 9 as soon as possible, so go get changed."

"DR 9?" I asked.

"Delivery Room," the nurse said a little impatiently, "room nine. It's down the hall." As she hurried off, I felt myself beginning to sweat. *What? I'm gonna be present while a baby is being delivered?* My last couple appointments had been in doctors' offices, but not in a delivery room!

For a second, I thought about calling the agency to tell them that I didn't feel qualified enough—but I decided to take on the challenge instead.

I trusted that I had memorized most of the medical terminology from the exam, and I was prepared with my medical term dictionary in case any words came up that I didn't know. But most importantly, I knew that if I didn't feel capable of doing the job, I could always call to ask for someone else more qualified to either help me or take over.

"Roberta, this is Carla," one of the nurses said slowly, gesturing to me and then back to the woman lying on the delivery bed in front of me. She gripped my hand tightly through her contractions, and I felt like the bones in my hand might break. "Carla will be interpreting for you today." I nodded and tried to smile.

"*Hola, Roberta,*" I said as warmly as I could. "*No se preocupe, todo va a estar bien.*"

As I expected, translating during a birth was intense. After hours of difficult labor, and relaying messages back and forth between Roberta and her medical team, her doctors noticed something unusual on their equipment.

"The baby is breech," the obstetrician said quickly. "We'll need to do a C-section. Carla, please explain to her." Given how serious and time sensitive the procedure was, I was forced to explain to Roberta while the doctor in the room was talking, once again feeling pushed further than I thought I could go.

The anesthesiologist gave Roberta a spinal tap to numb her from the waist down while she gripped my hand tightly, and they wheeled her to an operating room, as I hurriedly changed into scrubs and put on a surgical mask. The cacophony of the previous moment was replaced by an eerie quiet and the rhythmic beeps of two heartbeats on the cardiograph. *Please don't let there be too much blood*, I whispered to myself. *Please don't let me faint.* Sweat was beading on the obstetrician's brow as he dipped his surgical instruments behind a covering, handing his bloodied tools to nurses nearby for sanitization, along with plenty of used gauze.

In the heat of the moment, I thought I heard the surgeon cutting through the top layers of skin, which reminded me of ripping clothes. The doctor had warned me that I might feel lightheaded, but to my surprise I didn't; instead, I was fascinated by what the surgeons were doing.

Finally, after what seemed like an eternity (though it hadn't been more than a few minutes), the obstetrician produced a beautiful, screaming baby boy from under the covering and relief swept over the room. It was an incredible, shining moment—and there was so much blood that the father nearly fainted.

"Congratulations, sir," one of the nurses said warmly, washing the newborn. "You're a father!" All three members of the family embraced and shed tears of happiness. Though seeing it all through had made me convinced that I didn't want to have kids for a *long* time, I knew I would never forget the look in Roberta's eyes upon seeing her new baby.

After the nurses had dressed the baby and the father had been escorted from the room, I sat there in a daze. I hadn't anticipated how profound and intimate my interpreting job would be or how I would be involved in life-changing experiences with people.

"Hey, Carla," the obstetrician said, seeming to grin under his surgical mask. "You want to come see this?" He was holding up surgical thread and a needle, wiggling them in the air slightly.

"Sure," I said, not sure whether to be flattered or disturbed. The doctor waved me over, and I watched him sew Roberta's abdomen together stitch by stitch and layer by layer, not sure how my life had suddenly opened up so quickly. I never imagined that after less than a year after arriving in America, I would be interpreting for a surgeon and earning three times the minimum wage, without a high school diploma.

Again, I thought of my dad reminding me throughout childhood how grateful I should've been for learning English at a private school. *Yes, Dad, I know,* I had always said—but only as an adult did it really sink in. Thanks to my parents' early efforts, I had this job and was making a life in America. I was very proud of my new job. I felt so secure and stable that my plans to move to Canada were quickly dissipating from my mind.

Since I didn't have many other responsibilities and I wanted to learn as much as possible, I started saying yes to virtually every appointment that came my way. I didn't want to keep my hosting job, but I wanted to be sure I could make a living from interpreting first before letting it go.

On a typical day, I would get a call from the interpreting agency at midnight—when the on-staff interpreters' shifts ended—saying that someone who spoke Spanish had just come into the emergency room and the nurses needed an interpreter. Whenever that happened, I would get out of bed and drive down there for a few hours before driving home, showering as fast as I could, and then driving back to the restaurant for my shift.

About a month into juggling both jobs, it was clear that what I was doing was unsustainable. My energy was dropping, I had dark circles around my eyes and felt exhausted all the time. Still, I had some lingering fears about leaving a steady job to become a full-time freelancer.

When I finally got the courage to get out of my comfort zone, I broached the subject with Alec. He didn't support my idea.

"We're still living with my family, Carla," he said anxiously. "What if you quit, your interpreting shifts dry up and then you can't pay your part of the rent? How will it look if we're living here and not doing our fair share?" It was true that we all split the rent, utilities, groceries and other expenses five ways, but I intended to hold up my end of that arrangement.

"I'm still going to be able to pay rent," I replied. "If things don't work out, I'll just get another job as a hostess!"

"I don't think it's a good idea for you to leave your hostess job," Alec insisted. "We have way too many expenses and you not having a steady paycheck makes me nervous." Alec and I were both bad with finances; he had recently purchased his dream car, the Ford F150 pickup truck, and between the monthly car payment, insurance and gas, it cost almost half of our salary—and whatever was left over, we both tended to spend.

Even if he had some real concerns, Alec's lack of support for me choosing a job that made the best use of my skills and paid better was starting to irritate me. I needed a masculine energy that could instill more confidence in me, not plant more fears.

"Relax," I said finally. "You're not going to have to pay for me. If you don't take risks, you can't win or lose, you just stay stuck in the same place. I have to do this, but trust me, it will be okay."

For all of the back and forth we had about me quitting, I couldn't deny the simple fact: interpreting was where I saw the most opportunity. While working at the restaurant had been a great stepping stone, I didn't want it to be my permanent job. Besides, I didn't like the working conditions very much, and I didn't see a future there.

Finally, after juggling both jobs for the rest of the month, I took my leap of faith and quit the restaurant to focus on free-lancing as an interpreter full time.

As I soon learned, the interpreting industry had a very streamlined process. Generally speaking, each hospital only had one or two full-time interpreters of their own, because it was too expensive to keep many more on their payroll (plus you couldn't keep enough interpreters on staff to cover every language you might need).

The biggest interpreting companies in the area had standing contracts with big hospitals and subcontracted their people to them. It meant that working for one of those compa-nies had advantages and disadvantages. On the plus side, there was always a steady supply of work and interpreters didn't need to try and build their own relationships and infrastructure to get paid. Still, it also meant that you owed your time and schedule to someone else—and they were always taking a cut.

After my first batch of assignments, I got my first monthly paycheck of around $3,000—and I was elated. As a hostess, I made less than half that working three times as much! I was so happy that I bought myself a VW Beetle. My dream car when I was a teenager was to have a new, green version, but I settled for a used, black one that I could afford. All the same, it still felt magical—and I felt more independent now that Alec didn't have to drive me around anymore.

After about six months of taking assignments, I started thinking about the possibility of taking my earnings even further. *What if I opened my own agency?* I dared myself to dream. If Lucio had done it, maybe he could help me get started on the paperwork I would need to complete. It would be risky, because I knew that once I told the big agency that I was going to start covering appointments on my own, I probably wouldn't be their first choice of interpreter to call anymore. Instead, I would become their competition.

But if I pulled it off and got clients on my own, I would keep the additional 30 percent that the agency kept, while having more control over my schedule. Though I knew I needed to keep taking them, I was already starting to feel worn out by so many night shifts—they were a gold mine, since most interpreters didn't want to do them. Once again, I explained my thought process to Alec, and once again, he wasn't overly supportive.

"You only just got the hang of this," he said. "Now you want to take on these huge companies? Based on what you're telling me, they basically have a monopoly already, so how are you going to do that?"

"I'm not going to compete with them directly," I said patiently. "There's enough work for everyone. I'm just not going to do as much work directly with hospitals." As I explained, my plan would be to target small clinics without contracts with the big agencies, and I was only going to take L&I appointments, which were easier to bill than other state insurances. I knew there were businesses like that just from driving around town.

"With enough persistence, I think I can my find my own clients," I said. "I'm confident I can figure it out."

"What do you mean figure it out?" he shouted. "You're only 19 years old, Carla, and you've only been an interpreter for less than a year. You don't have a plan!" The more Alec and I talked about business and growth, the more our conversations ended poorly.

I now understood how most agencies got their clients. Basically, someone would get injured at work, and their employer would send that person to the hospital. For any longer interactions they might have with medical staff, the hospitals would send requests to the big agencies in the Tri-Cities, who would then send medical interpreters to work those appointments.

Alec was right: those big agencies *did* have a relative local monopoly on interpreting services—but only at big hospitals, and in effect, only for billing medical insurance companies. I also knew that *after* many of those workers went to the hospital, their health and recovery stories didn't end there.

Sometimes, a worker's injuries or health issues were bad enough that they would cause other related problems—whether they were psychological issues or additional medical issues you could treat outside of a hospital, at a smaller clinic or a specialized facility. Those places needed interpreters too, and they had a lot more room to compete.

More and more, my conversations with Alec were leaving me frustrated. While I didn't have a play *just yet,* all I wanted was his support and for him to believe in me. I was so used to my mom encouraging me and supporting me in most of my plans and ideas, that it was hard to not find that same support in the person I was sharing my life with. But I didn't let the idea dissipate just like that. Instead, I called the only person I thought could help me: Lucio.

"Hi Lucio," I said. "I have a question for you. If I had the wild idea of starting my own interpreting agency, would you be willing to guide me through the process?"

3

VIBRATION

"Nothing rests; everything moves; everything vibrates."

—THE KYBALION

Following our conversation, Lucio agreed to teach me about running my own agency based on what he had learned trying and failing to start his own. Since the paperwork was much easier than I thought, I realized the hardest part of starting a business: finding the right name. Finally, after filling out the online application and paying $25 for a business license, my agency, The Language Spot, was born.

"I can teach you about the paperwork and show you how to bill," he explained, "but you should know that there are three other smaller agencies in the area that only cover L&I appointments, and they fight each other for slots. They've been in the industry for a decade, and they're not going to like you stepping in to compete with them. It's part of why my agency didn't work out."

What he was saying made sense. Even with the limited interpreting experience I had, I'd already seen how much conflict there was between agencies about which clients belonged to whom, who could go to which clinic and so on.

Although L&I rules indicated that patients could use whatever interpreter they wanted as long as they were certified, the clinics still formed relationships with small agencies on their own and tended to call agencies directly when they needed interpreters. The result was that all the interpreters in the area knew which clinics had established relationships with whom, so they tended not to interfere with one another's businesses. It also meant that all the interpreters knew one another, and they tended to move freely between different agencies to fill appointments.

Luckily, I noticed that there was one local clinic called Pasco Worker Care that didn't have any firm contracts or relationships in place. After visiting and having a conversation with the receptionists, I learned that they had disliked the conflict between the competing agencies so much that they had decided to give any agency who dropped off a business card at their front desk an opportunity to interpret for their clients. It was also fortunate that this clinic was one of the very few emergency walk-in clinics for injured workers, so they tended to have a lot of open appointments that small agencies could compete over.

In general, the clinic's strategy was to go through the list of all the agencies to see who was available the soonest; typically, they preferred interpreters who could arrive within 15 minutes of a call, which was doable since the town was so small. I knew that competing over those slots would be difficult, though not impossible.

Since I only lived 10 minutes away from the emergency walk-in clinic, I decided I would do anything within my power to get there faster than anyone else, and would secure that relationship by getting to know the secretaries and the front-of-house staff. Even if I couldn't close any deals with them right away, I needed them to know my name and who I was. Eventually, if something fell through or there was an opening, I would rush over as fast as I could.

When they began to call me, I said yes to everything and made myself available all the time, even if it sometimes meant leaving in the middle of a social event. I would even get up early every morning even when I didn't have appointments, just to be available and on call if something did come up.

In the process of trying to win the clinic over, I started to realize why so many open appointments were coming up. Many of the existing agencies were using paper agendas to plan things, which made it very easy to forget appointments or forget to schedule follow-ups (the latter of which became my bread and butter). To have an advantage over them, I utilized electronic systems and learned Google Calendar inside and out, so that I would never miss an appointment.

After showing up again and again, the clinic grew to like me so much that my agency was the one covering most (if not all) of their appointments. I got so busy that Lucio offered to help me fill some of my appointments when he wasn't working his other part-time job as an on-staff interpreter at the hospital.

"L&I appointments will pay about $47 an hour," he said, "and most agencies pay their subcontractors $25 an hour, but I figure I can charge you $28, since I have more experience, with a minimum of a one-hour appointment at a time?" What he was saying made sense and still left me a good margin. And after all, it was thanks to him that I was in the business, so paying him more seemed reasonable.

Having Lucio help me meant that I could cover twice as many appointments, and with his help, I spent most of my day at the emergency walk-in clinic while he covered other appointments in different parts of town.

As the business kept growing, I started looking for even more interpreters to hire. One of the first was Maria, a good friend of Lucio's whom he knew from working at the hospital and who was also fully certified. He introduced the two of us at a restaurant one night and she smiled broadly, running up to me for a huge hug.

"Oh my gosh," she practically shouted, while I tried to squirm out of her grasp. "So great to meet you. I searched you and your photos up on Facebook and was shocked to see how much we look alike. I feel like we could pass for twins!"

"Twins?" I said, confused. "I don't know, maybe?"

"From now on, I'm going to call you sister!" she said with a big smile. Maria's energy was imposing, even though we barely knew each other. She was loud and over the top; still, she seemed like a capable interpreter, so I figured I'd be able to work with her.

The next hire was Bella, my ex-co-worker from the restaurant who had introduced me to Lucio. We had both learned about becoming interpreters from him at the same time, but she'd waited a bit longer to get her license. After seeing the high earning potential, she decided to finally take the tests so she could take on some part-time work.

Through my shifts at one of the clinics, I met Krystal, who was a physical therapy aide there and who also spoke perfect English and Spanish. I liked her vibe, and whenever I saw her at work, I would try to talk to her. As a result, we gradually became close friends and started having deeper conversations.

"I've always been interested in becoming an interpreter," she said, "but the people I've talked to said there's way too much competition right now. It seems that most interpreters are not willing to share more information with me."

"No way, you should go for it!" I replied. I knew Krystal provided excellent customer service and would make an incredible interpreter, so I told her that if she got certified, we could work together; as I had already seen firsthand, there was more than enough business to go around.

After explaining everything to them, both Bella and Krystal took the interpreting exam and both of them passed the written test—which was enough to earn their provisional licenses—but only Krystal eventually passed the oral exam and was fully licensed and eligible for a provider number. Though I really wanted to use Bella, I knew I couldn't give her L&I appointments until she passed the oral portion of the exam.

"You could still start giving her appointments before L&I issues her a provider number," Lucio suggested. "If you want, you can use my number to bill for her appointments in the meantime, since I'm fully certified." As he explained, all I would need to do is fill out a voucher with all her information and have her sign it—the only thing that would be amiss is that I'd be using Lucio's number on it instead of hers.

I knew it was a risk to fudge the paperwork, but I was getting busier and needed all the help I could get. *Bella is capable*, I thought, *and she'll pass the oral test eventually—this is just a short-term solution to keep things going in the meantime.* Sure enough, a few months later, she retook the oral exam and passed.

As I quickly found out, having other interpreters working with me besides myself was a risk. Sometimes, L&I denied claims altogether, and although I wasn't obligated to do so, I would still compensate my interpreters for appointments out of my own pocket to avoid them declining to work for me in the future. In a sense, the extra margin I made on my subcontractors was a way of ensuring that I always had an extra cushion for all the expenses the business incurred.

Things were moving in the right direction, and I knew I was on the right track a couple years into the business when in 2010, I got a call from one of the secretaries with whom I'd networked and landed one of my first great clients: Dr. Leenards.

I had heard about Dr. Leenards from some of the other interpreters and how particular he was about whom he chose to work with. The rumor was that he only used one interpreter for all of his work, but the interpreter couldn't always cover all the appointments he needed. He knew that he needed to expand slightly and a referring clinic recommended me to him.

On the day of my first appointment, and with little other information to go on, I got ready and drove to an address across town. Though I was used to driving to hospitals, this time I found myself in front of someone's house in a residential neighborhood.

After parking, I knocked on the door and a gentle-looking man in his 80s opened it. In the background, I could see his wife hunched over a cutting board in the kitchen with the faucet running. Confused, I quickly double-checked the address. *This can't be the place*, I thought, now embarrassed.

"Oh, I'm sorry," I said quickly, "I think I have the wrong address. I'm looking for Dr. Leenards?"

"Ah, you're the interpreter from the agency!" he said with a bright smile. "My office is through the backdoor. But please, come right this way!" With that, he swung the door all the way open and led me through the front room.

The upstairs of his house was beautifully decorated and had a warm and welcoming feeling about it, and as I walked through, he introduced me to his wife, who looked up from her cooking and waved. Finally, he led me downstairs into his office, which was just as warm but with a more professional appearance.

As he introduced himself, he explained that he had previously been a monk in Brazil, where he had met his wife when he was in his 60s. He had gotten malaria while he was there, and health complications led to him returning to the US to get treatment. After that, he stayed, got his doctorate in psychology and opened up his own energy psychology practice.

In my first session with him, he sat me down in a chair near his patient, who was a Latina woman wearing loose, worn clothing. A tractor had accidentally run into her, injuring her back. Although her physical wounds had healed a few months after the accident (according to medical doctors), her mental state hadn't. She was in a state of deep depression, and the sound of anything like a tractor would trigger feelings of fear, anxiety and helplessness, making it a challenge to return to work.

As I soon learned, though Dr. Leenards did some talk therapy, most of his practice was dedicated to working on clients' energy fields, using tapping techniques and other practices I had never heard of or seen before, such as earthing, sound healing, kinesiology and muscle testing.

After hearing the client describe her physical injury and how it was affecting her life, Dr. Leenards had her close her eyes and breathe.

"Everything vibrates," he explained. "We are all energy, simply moving at varying rates. Today I'm going to teach you how to influence those vibrations by changing your mental state." It was one of the first times I'd heard anybody talk about energy and vibration in real life outside of my mom! Though she had taught me about the law of attraction since I was a kid, I still hadn't connected all the dots about how thoughts, energy and our reality were connected.

From that first session, it was clear that Dr. Leenards understood the connections between those things very well. He was using both art and science to help heal people by focusing on their energy and their thoughts. As I took more of his appointments, he quickly became one of my favorite clients.

"You believe your limitations are all in your body," he would tell his clients, "but so many of them are only in your mind. While you work on healing your body in the physical plane, we will also work on healing your energy on the mental plane. You've heard the phrase, 'I think, therefore, I am,' or the phrase 'mind over matter.' What those things really mean is that the body tends to manifest whatever the mind believes."

As he explained, any and all manifestations of thought and emotion had their own corresponding rate and mode of vibration. If someone felt sad, for example, the energy in their body was vibrating at a lower frequency.

As a consequence, that frequency would tend to attract more negative or sad things. Since everything emitted energy, whether positive or negative, and since we could control what kind of energy we sent out into the universe, to a large extent, we could determine the outcome of our own life experiences.

"To vibrate at a higher level," he told his patients, "you have to find the lesson within the challenges you face and integrate it. Doing this will help you see things with more grace, love and understanding."

Whenever he talked, I would lean in, absorbing as much information and wisdom as I possibly could. As I learned from him, more of my childhood started to make sense. I could see why my mom was always in such a blissful state, and why my dad constantly suffered from depression and anxiety. She would always try to see the bright side of things, while my dad focused on the negative. After everything I'd been through leaving Mexico and trying to establish myself in America, it felt like Dr. Leenards's words were as much for me as they were for his patients.

One day when I met him at his door for another appointment, he had a wide-eyed look on his face.

"Carla!" he said excitedly, putting a hand on my shoulder and ushering me inside. "You won't believe what just happened to me." He began to explain that just moments before I had shown up at his door, he had had a vision while staring out the window.

"I was in the Amazon," he said quietly. "I was sitting in a circle looking around at shamans and aborigines with long hair covering their faces. They were playing drums and trying to send a message I couldn't understand." I nodded, not sure exactly where the story was going.

"Then a moment later, the hair moved away from one of their faces—and the face underneath was deformed," he said, pausing thoughtfully before continuing. "I got frightened and was about to run away from the circle when one of the aborigines whispered in my ear, 'Don't be afraid; the outside is just a shell. We are all *one* love, and we are all *one* universal vibration.' But it wasn't a dream! I could see myself sitting in the circle from above. It was an out-of-body experience, and then you knocked on the door."

I had never seen Dr. Leenards open up so much before. What he had just told me was a little bit puzzling, but the energy of his message stayed with me throughout our multiple sessions that day. When it was almost time to part ways, I thanked him for what he'd shared and for all of his lessons.

"It's always so great spending time with you, Dr. Leenards," I said. He smiled warmly.

"You're a bright woman, Carla," he said. "Have you thought about going back to school?"

"No," I replied. "I haven't thought about it much recently."

"What's stopping you from it?" he asked with a big smile.

"I don't know," I said. "It's been five years since I stepped into a classroom, and I would feel embarrassed about being so much older than my classmates." I suddenly remembered that Dr. Leenards had started school when he was in his 60s. *Oops,* I thought.

"Remember what you hear me telling my patients," he said. "If you put your efforts into something with the right mindset, there are no limits to what you can do."

With his words still ringing in my ears, I drove home, pondering what I would choose to do if there really were no limits.

4

ENERGY

"If you want to find the secrets of the universe, think in terms of energy, frequency, and vibration."

—NIKOLA TESLA

After just a few years in business, The Language Spot's revenue had grown to around $60,000 a year, the same as what someone with a college degree could earn—and a *huge* improvement from the $13,000 or so a year I had made while working at the restaurant. With all the appointments I was getting from all the clinics I was providing services to, I had enough work to keep me busy for eight hours a day, while still giving my three interpreters a handful of additional appointments each week.

As my business picked up, my relationship with my dad was also gradually improving. He had come to visit me in Pasco, and in a sense, it felt like the distance between us had helped us heal somewhat. After seeing how well things were going, he was confused about our living situation.

"Carla, you're making good money," my dad said to me over the phone one day. "Why are you still living with Alec's parents?"

At first, we'd been living with Alec's parents to save on expenses, but now that we were financially stable enough to move out, he didn't want to. Instead, we were spending our money quickly—particularly on a nice, convertible Audi TT which we'd traded in my Beetle for. Although Alec had originally bought the Audi for himself, after a year of convincing him that having me drive the F-150 around town to so many different appointments was making our gas bills too expensive, he finally agreed to trade cars with me.

Alec and I didn't have very good habits when it came to saving our money. In fact, we loved to spend it, particularly on trips to Vegas. It was how we began dreaming about a new business idea after one particular trip to the city of lights.

"Imagine if we opened a bar that was kind of Vegas-style, with lights, good music and good cocktails," he said. "Around here, there's almost nothing like that." Alec was still working at Torito's and had finally been promoted from busser to server and bartender. He was gaining experience on how to make cocktails, and he was good at it.

"That's true," I pondered. "The Tri-Cities could really use an upscale martini bar." As we discussed the idea more, we wondered if it might really be possible to pull off a business like that together. Opening an interpreting agency hadn't required a lot of money—all I'd needed was a cell phone, computer, printer and my availability. Opening a bar would require capital, a liquor license and God knew what else. Still, the idea felt like an exciting one to do together, and even more exciting was the idea of Alec getting out of his comfort zone to explore his higher potential. Since I already had some experience starting and scaling a business, I could handle at least some of the paperwork and financing—and for whatever I didn't know, I was up to the challenge of learning it.

We determined that we had $10,000 available on our credit cards, and since Alec had worked with his dad in Mexico in a wood shop, they would be the ones to build the furniture. As we researched on YouTube, we realized that all we would need for a glowing bar was a wood foundation, plexiglass and a few hundred dollars in LED strip lights.

By the end of the week, we were settled on the idea of opening a martini bar together—but since Alec still didn't speak any English, most of the work that had to be done at the beginning would be up to me, and there were a lot more obstacles in our way than I realized.

First, we started looking for locations nearby to determine how much money we would need to actually start our business. One was too expensive, another was too small and a third would've been perfect, if not for the cost of renovations it would need. Finally, after a few weeks of searching, we found a location that was as good as we could get for our needs: the right size, a good location and a reasonable price of $3,500 a month to rent.

The business that had been in the location before us was a photo studio, so we knew right away that we would need to do renovations. The Department of Health required two bathrooms, so on top of the cost of adding a kitchen, we would need to build another bathroom as well. After some rough math, we figured it might take $20,000 to do everything we needed to do —twice as much as we'd anticipated.

After searching online and talking to friends, I learned about the Small Business Administration (SBA), which lent money to entrepreneurs at low rates for their business ventures.

I also realized that in order to get funding, I needed to write up a business plan. Since I had never written one before, I spent hours on the internet figuring out how to do it, often waking up at 4 or 5 in the morning before work to research and put my energy in motion. Fortunately, the place we were renting hadn't been rented for a year, so we had some time to figure things out.

When the time came for an appointment, I gathered all my papers and headed down to the local SBA office to meet with a representative. I felt confident about all the work I'd done and everything I'd put into our business plan—even though I'd found out through my research that restaurants only had a 20 percent success rate and that 80 percent failed within their first five years of opening. *There's no reason why we can't be in that 20 percent*, I thought.

"Everything looks like it's in order," the woman in the conference room said, her eyes taking a close inventory of everything on the paperwork. "But it looks like you forgot to add in your social security number here." At that, my stomach dropped. *Not again.*

"I don't have a social security number," I replied, "but I do have an ITIN. I opened my other business with it, so I should be able to apply with that, right?" My legal identifier in the US was this Individual Tax Identification Number, which the government gave to resident and non-resident aliens so that they could still pay taxes. The woman frowned slightly.

"I see," she said. "I'm sorry, but we can't give SBA loans to anyone who doesn't have a social security number." I sighed and nodded that I understood before collecting my papers and walking back to my car in the parking lot. *There has to be another way to make this work*, I thought. Soon after, the time came to call the owners of our intended location, who were a young couple from Seattle who owned multiple commercial buildings.

"We're very interested in moving forward," I explained, "but we just need a little more time to figure out how we're going to make this work."

"Well, why don't we help you out?" the husband said.

"Yeah!" his wife seconded. "We can come down from Seattle to meet you and talk everything through."

Sure enough, the couple drove to Pasco, took Alec and I out to dinner and essentially gave us a free coaching session on how to get started. We talked about the costs of renovations and determined that adding a kitchen and a bathroom would eat up our entire $10,000, without leaving enough for furniture, inventory, point-of-sale equipment or any money for reserves.

We hadn't thought through how expensive the entire project would be, but after seeing our passion and determination, the couple decided to make us an offer.

"Why don't we do this," the husband said finally. "We can extend you a loan for $10,000 without interest so you can do the renovations, so long as we get paid in our first year in business." As they explained, they believed in our vision and also agreed that the Tri-Cities needed a bar like the one we were describing. "We can even introduce you to a contractor who is doing renovations at other office spaces in the same strip mall."

After accepting their offer, we met with their contractor at our new space and explained our vision to him.

"What's your budget for the project?" he asked.

"Ten thousand dollars," I replied.

"You have champagne taste on a beer budget," he said, laughing at how much we wanted to accomplish with such little money. "But I'll make that work. I'll give you a deal since you are both young and need a hand. I can charge you $10,000, but you have to pay up front, so I can start working on this immediately and rent costs don't creep up on you."

Happy with the deal we'd made, we gave him the check for $10,000 that our landlords had given us—and the contractor promptly disappeared with it after only working at our location for a week. When we inspected the site, we saw that all he had done was open a trench for where the plumbing would go and nothing else. We were now $10,000 short with a lease in place, and rent was running.

After explaining what had happened to Alec's dad, he offered to lend us $10,000 to pay back once the bar started producing. I reached out to my dad as well.

"I can lend you $10,000," he said. "But I'll need a contract in place for 10 percent interest a year, with monthly installments beginning the first month the bar is open." We both agreed, and with the rest of our money, we found a new contractor and explained what had happened to us. Clearly, he felt bad for us.

"I'm sorry to hear what you two have been through," he said. "I can charge you $10,000 to finish up the plumbing and electrical, but you two will have to do the labor on the rest." It meant that we would need to build everything and put in the drywall and tile ourselves, despite having never done it before. Even so, we were grateful for the help, and we agreed.

Since we couldn't afford to hire help after losing half of our start-up money, Alec and I started watching instructional YouTube videos and reaching out to friends who could help us build on the weekends. During the week, I would watch hours of videos on how to lay tile and how to frame out a wall. Then, on the weekends, our friends would put what we'd learned into action, and we'd pay them back with pizza and beer.

We were making great progress, but the total costs of everything were closer to $40,000 than $20,000—and even with money coming in from Language Spot, juggling everything was becoming difficult and stressful.

The hours I was working were extreme, my energy was draining and my relationship with Alec was strained. In order to focus on the bar renovations full-time, Alec had quit his job at Torito's—but instead of using the mornings to get things done quickly, he woke up late, went to the gym and waited for me to come back from work at 5 pm to start on the renovations at the bar.

One of the few respites I had was the time I spent at work. When I wasn't working on opening the bar, I was spending a lot of time with Dr. Leenards—often many sessions a day for three or four hours, since he only worked with me and one other interpreter.

Everything else in my life was chaotic, but my time with Dr. Leenards was always peaceful and rejuvenating. I interpreted for multiple different psychologists, but I saw that Dr. Leenards's patients showed steadier improvement using his unconventional techniques than other patients who used more traditional methods.

Dr. Leenards had an intense interest in everyone who came into his house. Before starting treatment, the first thing he would do was ask his patients were eating or if they had anything toxic in their home environment that might be affecting them. In addition to things like laundry soap and chemicals like aspartame in Diet Coke, he explained that even nightshade plants—such as tomatoes, eggplants, potatoes and peppers—could cause people inflammatory problems as well. It was incredible to see his patients reduce their pain just by cutting some of those foods out of their diets!

His lessons about the power of visualization had been in my head since I was a teenager. It was something my mother and I had always talked about: charting your own course, picturing how you would get there and calling in the spiritual energy you needed to make your dreams a reality. Now, thinking about my life in America and my growing business, I could see I was right on the cusp of realizing those dreams, even if it was challenging.

After my disappointing run-in with the SBA, other people I'd met in the restaurant business told me to brace myself for the same thing to happen when the time came to get a liquor license. According to them, there was no way they would give a license to someone who didn't have an SSN. But they didn't know how badly I wanted it.

I looked online and did extensive research to see what was possible. As I read in the fine print, there was nothing that said you *couldn't* get a license if you only had an ITIN, which was enough hope for me.

After filling out all the paperwork and submitting it, I started calling the liquor board and any other help numbers I could, trying as hard as I could to establish a relationship and show my tenacity. After months of follow-ups, the day I'd been waiting for finally came: the liquor board approved our license!

With that in place and all our renovations finished, we were finally ready. After almost two months of raising money and renovating, White Buddha Lounge was officially open for business.

5

PLEASURE AND PAIN

"The aim of the wise is not to secure pleasure, but to avoid pain."

—ARISTOTLE

Though Alec and I had no savings and were still carrying about $10,000 in credit card debt from all the money we'd put into the bar, the business itself began bringing in cash quickly upon opening, and the local community was embracing us. Local newspapers wrote about us, and we were even interviewed on the local news! We were starting to steadily pay down our debts—the only issue was between The Language Spot and the bar, I had been over-exerting myself and breaking my body down.

My relationship with Alec was beginning to strain, and my mistake was not putting my foot down on things that were not acceptable to me. Instead, we masked our issues by continuously drinking and partying—and my 21st birthday was no exception.

When the big night came, Alec and all my friends rented a limo for me to go nightclubbing. All night, we drove around drinking tequila and margaritas. We decided to drive to a bar in Umatilla which was in Oregon, about 30 minutes from where we lived, so we could enjoy the long ride. By the time we were on the way home, we were all a little sloppy.

"Are you okay, Carla?" Alec asked me, trying to steady me in the backseat. I was swaying a little too much as the limo made its turns around the city.

"I'm starting to feel it," I said a little loudly. Lucio overheard me and leaned in with a smile, squeezing both of our arms excitedly.

"I know the perfect remedy for this," he yelled. "Tacos!" Everyone else in the back of the limo cheered. After giving the driver some instructions, he made another turn and pulled into a wide parking lot. We got out to see we were in front of La Esperanza, a taco truck that was always busy no matter how late it was.

"What's up, girl?" Lucio purred, pushing his way up to an attractive woman in line who had her back turned to us. "You two need to meet! Carla, this is Yesenia." We both said hi to each other, but we weren't overly friendly. *I love her curly hair,* I thought, slightly intimidated.

"Nice ride to get tacos in," she said smiling, pointing at the limo.

"It's Carla's birthday!" Lucio announced. Before any other words came to me, Alec ran up behind us, clapped his hands on our shoulders and introduced himself as well.

"Alec, like the singer!" Yesenia said. Alec smiled widely. There was a Mexican version of *The Voice* with a popular singer on it named Alec, so it was a comment he got a lot—and he particularly liked getting it when it meant other girls were paying attention to him. Finally, the cashier handed Yesenia her box of tacos and she stepped out of line.

"Nice to meet you all," she said, turning slightly to me. "Happy birthday—and try not to spill on that Selena-style shirt, okay?" Suddenly self-conscious, I looked down at the puffy white top I was wearing, almost certain that I would ruin it while eating tacos.

"Thanks," I said, as she took a seat at a table far from us. We all went back to the limo with our food. Bella was with us and had noticed the interaction between Yesenia and me. Once we were back inside, she leaned towards me.

"Lucio told me that girl is a lesbian," she whispered with a smile and her eyebrows raised. It was just idle gossip, but I was surprised. *Most of the lesbian girls in town are not nearly as feminine as she was*, I thought.

Though our bar was doing well, the tension between Alec and I had never been higher. When we weren't working, we were drinking too much with friends, without a lot of time left to connect. When we were "connecting," it was usually by arguing about something.

I was beginning to suspect that he was being disloyal, since he was becoming more secretive than usual about his phone and his passwords. I was finally able to get ahold of his unlocked phone and found several messages of him flirting with a girl who was a regular at the bar, and several phone calls to a number I didn't recognize. When I dialed the number back, I realized it was for a strip club.

While life with the bar had made everything a lot more stressful, it was also very entertaining to be there and working the crowd. There was an attractive woman who was a regular at the bar who would flirt with me—and because Alec was already doing it, I let myself flirt back. On one occasion, she slipped me a napkin with her phone number on it and winked when I looked up. After she left, I threw away the napkin and didn't call her. I blushed at the interaction that we'd had together, which made me wonder why I had enjoyed it in the first place. By contrast, whenever a guy tried to flirt with me or give me his number, I was completely uninterested, which took me by surprise.

On another night, I noticed Lucio and his wife entering the bar with Yesenia and her girlfriend. Yesenia didn't say hi, but I noticed her. I knew there were some lesbians in town, and most of the time, I would see them in couples where one of them was more masculine and the other more femme. Seeing Yesenia and her girlfriend both dressed femme and attractive was a paradigm shift in the way I had stereotyped lesbian couples. Above all, it was making me realize that I was losing my attraction for Alec, which scared me.

Around the same time, my best friend Mariana was coming to visit in Pasco and planning to stay with Alec and me for a month or so. We had grown up together, and since I hadn't seen her since I'd left Guadalajara, I couldn't have been more excited for her visit. We both greeted her warmly when she arrived and went out together, but it didn't take long for her to notice that something was off between us. More specifically, something was off with me.

One day, we were both at a restaurant and went to the bathroom together, starting a conversation between our stalls.

"What's going on with you?" she asked me. "You can't hide from me, I know something is wrong."

"Things aren't going well with Alec," I said, "I'm afraid I'm at a point where I don't know if I want to fix things or just leave him. All I know is I'm not happy anymore." As I thought about it, my interactions with Alec had only been getting worse. His sarcastic jokes about how my opinion on certain matters shouldn't count since I didn't finish high school were more frequent, and he was getting more controlling about how I dressed and spoke. One time after leaving a gathering with our friends, he told me that he thought I talked and laughed too loudly—and that I should try not to talk as much. He was making me self-conscious about myself in so many ways, including my physical appearance.

Since Mariana always gave such great advice, I was expecting something neutral and balanced from her in response. Instead, she went a different route.

"Baby, I am glad you finally opened your eyes and realized it!" she exclaimed. "I honestly thought it was only going to take you a few months of dating him to realize it, but when I saw years pass and you stayed with him, I just made peace with it, like your dad did. Still, you have never fully been yourself with him."

The more she explained, the more I thought of my mom and dad, and how her voice had quieted over the years as a result of not establishing clear boundaries with my dad from the beginning, and I knew I was repeating the same pattern.

"He doesn't let you be yourself," Mariana continued. "You're probably not happy because he's trying to mold you the way *he* wants you to be, and the real you is trapped inside some-where. He's not treating you the way you deserve. Every time he makes one of those passive-aggressive comments to you, it feels like a punch in the stomach."

As weeks passed, Mariana and I talked more about my rela-tionship, and I explained how difficult things had been. Alec and I had been dating for seven years, but the majority of the friends we had together in Pasco were his friends first, and I was pretty sure I'd lose them if we were to separate. On top of it all, the only family support I had in town was Alec's, and I was certain I would lose it if we separated. Since we had lived together for five years, I had developed a deep regard and appreciation for them.

Alec's family were beginning to notice that things were more tense than ever between us. To make matters worse, whenever Alec got upset at me, his mom would change her energy towards me to hint at her disapproval. There was almost no privacy in our relationship since we all lived together and knew each others' business. It didn't help that Alec was his mom's favorite child and didn't want us to move out on our own, all of which I confessed to Mariana.

"Why are you letting all of this happen?" she asked, aghast. "If there were love and respect between the two of you, I would tell you that it was worth fighting for your relationship. But baby, I'm sorry, he doesn't respect you. Every time I ask you why you have bruises on your wrists, you start making excuses. I don't think this is the love you deserve."

Exploring the topic only brought me more and more anxiety, but Mariana was doing her best to calm me down and give me strength. As she explained, she had just graduated from college and didn't have a job yet. Because of that, she wasn't tied down to anything, and she could help me.

"I'll stay here for as long as you need me to," she said. "I can even be your roommate and help you with the expenses if that's what you need. Just know that I'm here for you."

One night soon after, Alec and I were in our bedroom and I was upset with him for turning off his cell and not coming home until early in the morning—without even telling me that he was going out to party.

"I didn't have my charger with me and my phone died!" he yelled. "I was just keeping my friend company because they were cleaning the carpet at Torito's." Although Alec didn't work there anymore, his friend who was the manager did. Still, it seemed like every week, he was staying there late to keep his friend company because they had to "clean the carpet." What Alec didn't know, however, was that a waiter there told me that the carpets only got cleaned once a month. It was just another one of his lies.

"Okay, enough is enough," I said angrily. "I'm not happy with you anymore, and I'm leaving." As we started talking it through, I also told him that I thought I might be attracted to girls, which made him perk up a bit.

"Carla, that's a normal feeling," he said. "If this is mostly about that, I would even support you more." I declined; I knew I needed my own space and some time to think.

"I'm sorry, but no," I said. "Also, please don't tell anybody what I just told you. I need to think about it myself and to give it time before I talk about it.

With Mariana's support, I started looking for places and found an affordable two bedroom apartment that was going to be available in a month. In the time we had left together, I did my best to avoid Alec's mom and keep a low profile, though it was no use. During that time, Alec called my dad and told him that I was getting crazy ideas from Mariana—including being attracted to women.

With that, my dad called Mariana's dad and asked him to order his daughter to come home as soon as possible, foiling our plans to live together. With Mariana gone, I thanked her for her support and moved into the two bedroom apartment on my own, with plans of using the second bedroom as an office. Since I was making good money, I figured I could still afford it by myself.

At 22 years old, I was living by myself for the first time ever. Though I thought I'd finally have some space from Alec, it turned out that change didn't come so easily. Even apart, I was still waking up at 5 or 6 am, covering translating shifts for surgeries, sometimes finishing up to 12 hours later, and then going to the bar to work until close and doing it all over again. On the weekends, I didn't work in my interpreting business, but the hours at the bar were long—sometimes, we didn't finish until three or four in the morning.

Our separation didn't last long because without any support system around, he wore me down and talked me into giving us another chance. After that, he moved all his stuff from his parents' house into my apartment. Eventually, it felt like there wasn't even much love between us anymore; he was just too comfortable with me to let me go, and I was too uncomfortable with the idea of leaving. In no time, we had gone from being boyfriend and girlfriend to roommates-slash-business partners who occasionally slept together.

Though the bar consumed our nights and weekends, I sometimes ran into Yesenia from time to time through my social circle. I found myself drawn to her even if she was aloof towards me, always wondering what she was up to and intrigued by her lifestyle. She was an open and out lesbian and exuded confidence and authenticity. She had so much presence, no matter where she entered. Meanwhile, I was more confused than ever about my own love life and future.

As our bar kept growing, Alec and I took opposite shifts and saw each other less. Although we made some efforts to rekindle what we had, deep down we knew we were just clinging to one another and prolonging the inevitable.

Over the course of a year, we broke up and got back together another three or four times, unable to disentangle ourselves from one another. What we had was over, but we still felt trapped in the same patterns. In one of our many fights, I gave him an ultimatum.

"If you don't start respecting me," I said, "I'm going to end up meeting someone who does and it will be game over for you."

———————

Though the relationship between Alec and I was messier than it had ever been before, we still organized a party for the second anniversary of our bar and invited all our friends, even if I didn't particularly feel like celebrating. My attitude changed when I saw Yesenia sitting on one of the lounge sofas with Alec and Lucio. Upon seeing her, I sat right across from her, next to Alec.

"Congratulations, you two!" she beamed, toasting us with her martini. "Two years with a business is not easy." Alec gave a thin smile and raised his glass before turning his back to her.

"Thank you," I said sheepishly. "It's been a difficult time." At this, her face softened.

"I know what you mean," she replied. "I actually just made it to two years with my own business, so I know how hard it can be." As she explained, she had a small business selling car insurance and doing other people's taxes.

"Well, cheers and congratulations to you then!" I said, lifting my drink again. She smiled, and again, we clinked glasses. At that, she was about to stand up and go back to her seat when I found the courage to speak up.

"Why are you leaving so soon?" I asked. Yesenia stopped and turned around.

"Oh, I had just come to congratulate you two," she began, "but I can sit back down and stay for a while."

As the night went on, bodies swirled around us and Yesenia and I stayed put, talking about our interests, struggles and aspirations. As she explained, she had actually lived in Seattle for a while with Lucio, when he was trying to start an interpreting agency and she was going to the University of Washington— she had been the mysterious business partner Lucio had talked about! The conversation with her felt so easy. We could talk about anything and everything. She was funny, attractive, entertaining, smart and humble.

"So where are you originally from?" she asked.

"I'm from Guadalajara," I replied.

"My ex-girlfriend was from Guadalajara, too! The city is very pretty." *Oh,* I thought, *she no longer has a girlfriend.* I felt a swirl of attraction in my stomach. I couldn't believe that I had been seeing her face on and off at parties around Pasco for three years and had never gotten to know her until now. To my surprise, I was even feeling butterflies—it was a feeling of attraction I hadn't felt before.

Though we'd avoided each other for years, Yesenia and I had an instant connection, and after talking for a couple of hours, it felt like we had known each other for a long time. She seemed to trust me so quickly that we even discussed things I had only talked to Mariana about.

"It has been great talking to you," Yesenia said at the end of the night, "but I should probably get home." As she grabbed her bag and got up, I gave her a hug and watched her leave, starting to frown. To my surprise, I saw a text message from Yesenia about 30 minutes after she left with Lucio:

Carla, this is Yesenia. I am so sorry but we accidentally left without paying! I thought Lucio had paid, and he thought I paid, and it turns out neither of us did. I'm so embarrassed.

I smiled while typing out my reply.

Don't worry about it! It's on the house.

A moment later, I got another text:

Absolutely not! I'll swing by next weekend to pay.

From that moment on, Yesenia and I were texting non-stop. Though Alec and I still owned the bar together and were technically still together, I no longer had any feelings for him. I remembered what I told him once: "If you don't take care of me, one day, someone will come and show me more care than you do, and then it's going to be too late!"

As far as I could tell, that time seemed to be near. Although Yesenia and I were just friends at the beginning, I enjoyed our deep conversations and loved the way she looked at me. Ever since I'd been a girl, I had suspected I might be attracted to women, but it had been impossible to know for sure.

I'd briefly had a secret crush on one of the girl customers at our bar, though I knew nothing serious would come from it. Exploring a relationship like that in the culture I'd come from in Mexico would've meant being shunned or disowned; it just wasn't done easily. Still, I couldn't deny what I was feeling, even if it was making the distance between Alec and I even greater.

Yesenia came to the bar the next Friday, and it took my breath away to see her walk in. She was wearing a fitted blue dress with colorful high heels, her hair and make-up done perfectly. The entire thing made me so nervous that I ran to the back office.

"Carla, someone is looking for you," one of the bartenders yelled, knocking on the office door. With a deep breath, I came out and met Yesenia at the bar.

"I came to pay you back," she yelled. "And give me five

shots for my other friends! I convinced them to come here and have some drinks before we went out dancing." *I can't remember the last time I went out dancing and having fun,* I thought. Alec didn't like to dance—and we'd been working at the bar almost every single weekend for the last two years.

"So, when are you coming to my office so I can give you a quote for your car insurance?" she asked.

Sure enough, the next week, I came to her office to get my quote, dressing up nicely like she had when she came to pay me back. I also secretly brought a bottle of wine, which I left in the car just in case I got the guts to ask her if she wanted to share it with me after she closed her office for the day.

Although she couldn't find me a cheaper quote than what I was already paying, I still decided to switch over so I could have an excuse to see her more. After I signed the paperwork, she looked at her watch.

"Oh, it's 5 pm—time for happy hour," she said. "Want to grab a quick drink before you head back to work?" Alec wasn't going to like it; I knew he was going to be upset about me going out to have a drink with a friend (particularly a lesbian, since I'd already expressed curiosity about my attraction to girls before), but more so that it would mean showing up late to the bar. He didn't enjoy talking to our customers all that much, and since happy hour was our busiest time, I was typically the one who had to carry the conversations while he made drinks or chatted with his dad—who was our cook—in the kitchen. Still, I was tired of pleasing him—after all, it felt like he never did anything to please me.

After joining Yesenia for drinks nearby, we sipped our martinis and talked about life until eventually, the conversation turned to my recent discovery that I was attracted to women. At this, her eyebrows raised slightly.

"So, are you bisexual?" she asked.

"I don't like labels," I replied nervously. The truth was I wasn't ready to admit that I could potentially be described by a label other than "straight," though I didn't say so.

"You're cold!" she said, noticing that I was getting chills. "Let me give you my jacket." The bar was cold and I wasn't wearing a sweater, but when Yesenia rubbed her hand against my arm, my goosebumps only got more intense. I couldn't believe how deeply comforting her touch felt. I felt so drawn to her.

Yesenia and I kept texting and seeing each other for happy hours, while our desire to spend more time together grew. After about two weeks of this back and forth, Yesenia came to the bar and told me that she was going to Seattle that weekend for a Pride festival with some friends.

"You better not misbehave," I said, smiling. It was somewhere between flirting and letting her know how jealous I would be if she ended up meeting someone.

"Well, you and I are just friends, and you're with someone, so you can't really tell me how I should behave," she replied with a smirk on her face. *She's right*, I thought, feeling a pang of guilt, jealousy and desire all at once.

"I'm starting to have feelings for you," I blurted.

"The feelings are mutual," she said, "but you're with someone. You have to figure out what it is that you want first. You have to do things right, or I can't be more than a friend to you." After saying all that, she turned and walked toward the exit, and my stomach dropped.

The connection I was making with Yesenia was more real than anything I had felt in a long time, but I was still so afraid of breaking things off to explore my new feelings. The world around me came into sharp focus a few hours later when Alec came to the bar with our dinner. Whatever he had ordered didn't look good, but he wanted me to try it.

"No, thank you," I replied, pushing it away.

"I said to try it!" he said, raising his voice and throwing it impolitely onto my plate. For whatever reason, I could never find the courage to bring up the conversation of leaving Alec until we were already in the middle of a fight. I never wanted to feel guilty for leaving him, and so I always waited until a tense moment to broach the subject. With him throwing food on my plate, it suddenly felt like a perfect moment.

"Alec, I want to separate from you," I said abruptly. "This time once and for all."

"You've been spending too much time lately with that lesbian friend of Lucio's," he replied angrily. "Does she have anything to do with this?"

"It has more to do with the fact that there is no more love or respect between us," I said. "And it has to do with me figuring out who I am and why I feel attracted to women." After explaining my feelings a moment longer, we both cried and gave each other a hug.

"I have to admit that you're right," he said finally. "I'm not happy anymore either. Maybe this is for the best. I'll move my stuff out of the apartment and back in with my parents. We'll figure out the situation with the bar later." I felt so much relief hearing him say those words—although moving back in with his parents wasn't ideal, since they had just rented a new apartment in my complex directly across from mine so they could still stay close to Alec.

Even so, the way Alec had finally come around made me think that maybe a smooth transition into a new life would be possible. Unfortunately, time proved just how naive I was.

6

LOVE AND FEAR

"Everything you've ever wanted is on the other side of fear."

—GEORGE ADAIR

It was good to have finally pulled myself out of the vicious cycle that Alec and I had been in, and this time, it had felt more decisive. I was finally standing up for myself and not settling for less. I had found someone whom I thought might love me the way I didn't think anyone could: just the way I was, and not the way they wanted me to be.

Though I had hoped for a smooth transition into a new phase of life, I found myself in the depths of emotional and financial chaos instead. Alec and I were still in business together, and all of the paperwork was under my name, including all of the various lines of credit we'd taken out. We had to have a discussion over who would keep the bar and how we would disentangle ourselves from one another, hopefully in a way that wouldn't affect me negatively long-term.

"I don't think I can pay you out," Alec said simply. "I don't think there's a clean way to split it evenly down the middle." After talking it over dozens of different ways, we came to a fairly one-sided agreement: he would pay me $5,000 to walk away from the bar (to be paid in monthly installments since he didn't have the money available), and in exchange, Yesenia and I wouldn't ever step foot in the bar again.

As frustrated as I was that I'd be losing out on something I built, I didn't have the time or energy to fight about it anymore. I also knew the bar was everything to him—it was where he hung out with friends, and it was his only source of social status and income. The bar together represented my past, and though I was grateful for all the good things it had brought into my life, I was ready to let go of it. It was better to focus all of my energy on turning the page on the next chapter of life—especially because I was going through so much turmoil that I wasn't sure I would ever feel emotionally settled again.

Yesenia and I started seeing each other more regularly, and since Alec and his parents lived right in front of my apartment, they were all aware of what I was up to. Because we were in such close proximity, it also meant that Alec had gone back on what he'd said before about being okay with separating. Every so often, he would call me drunk late at night or even show up on my doorstep, asking for another chance to make things right.

It was hard to see him in so much pain, but deep in my heart, I knew that we couldn't keep repeating our cycle. It was hard to let go, but even if he loved me, he couldn't love me the way I wanted to be loved.

As I had feared, I lost nearly all of our mutual friends, since they sided with or supported Alec in the breakup. In Alec's eyes, everything had been fine between us and then one day, I went crazy, decided I liked girls and left him for Yesenia—at least, that was the story he was telling around town. Since our bar was popular and people knew who we were, rumors spread quickly, and people started turning their backs on me, no matter how friendly I was. Anyone who didn't block me on Facebook simply ignored me when they saw me out in public.

Still, a few friends remained, like Krystal and her husband Fonsi who had always supported me (and they had never really liked Alec, anyway). My other friend Tanya, whom I met through a mutual friend and was from a town near Guadalajara, also gave me her full support.

"Girl, the Tri-Cities is a small place, and people talk," she said. "It's not going to be easy to come out as gay, especially because so many people know who you and Alec are, but you have to stay true to yourself. People will talk for a while, but eventually, they'll forget."

Alec had already been going around telling people in town that I had left him because I was gay, even though I had explicitly told him that I wasn't ready to make that public yet. Still, I understood that he was hurt. Perhaps when he told me that separating was for the best, he didn't really believe that this time, it would be for good. Ultimately, I followed Tanya's advice. I would stay true to myself and follow my heart, which felt so warm and complete with Yesenia.

Despite all the drama, life with Yesenia was incredible. After a few weeks of spending time together as slightly more than friends, I came over to her house to cook *tacos de lengua en salsa verde*—tongue tacos in green sauce—which was a meal saved for special occasions in my family. Since we shared a similar background, it never occurred to me that she might not be into tongue tacos—and when she saw the giant tongue boiling on the stove, I could see the hesitation on her face.

"You don't like these?" I asked, trying not to giggle at the expression on her face. She steeled herself and swallowed once.

"Babe," she said, "for you, I'm more than willing to try them." When the time came to eat, she was surprised that she liked them and finished her whole plate—though she quickly requested that it not become a regular meal for the two of us.

Seeing her willingness to try new things with me, while being herself and at the same time letting me be myself in a harmonious exchange of energies, drove me crazy. The way she looked at me that night with such a loving and passionate gaze made me melt. Nobody had ever looked at me the way she did. It gave me goosebumps, and even if I wasn't ready to come out publicly, right there and then, I asked her to be my girlfriend.

In the meantime, things with Alec were getting harder and harder. I blocked his number and asked him not to come to my house in the middle of the night while drunk. One night, after noticing that I was gone for the weekend, he came in and inspected every corner of my house without telling me. When I came back and found out what happened, I changed all my locks and told him it was over.

Realizing how much unresolved pain I had (and how confused I was about my feelings), I told Yesenia that I had jumped into a relationship too soon, and that we needed to break up. She frowned.

"Are you sure?" she asked. I nodded sadly.

"Well, let's at least say our goodbyes with some tequila," she said. I nodded and we went to a bar around the corner from her office. Though we were only supposed to have a drink or two, we ended up having more than a few and staying to sing karaoke and cry together. As she explained, she had unresolved business with her own ex that she needed to take care of as well, so maybe it was for the best to take a break. *It's so strange,*

I thought. *Even during our breakup, things just flow so easily together.*

After our discussion, Yesenia left for Mexico for a couple of days to close her own chapter with her ex. Hearing about the conversation we'd had, Lucio offered his friendship in the best way he knew how: partying.

"Baby, you can't stay home by yourself crying," he said. "It's a Saturday night! Let's go out dancing!" Of course, I didn't decline the offer.

That night, Lucio and I were having a good time dancing bachata, when I saw Alec on the dance floor, stumbling over towards Lucio and me. *Fuck*, I thought. *Alec hates dancing— what is he even doing here?* When he got to us, he roughly pulled my arm.

"Carla, I need to talk to you," he said. Lucio tried to step in, but I stopped him.

"It's okay," I said, walking to the side of the dance floor to talk to Alec.

"Carla," Alec said, crying in the middle of the dance floor, "I just got diagnosed with cancer." I was in shock.

"What!?" I asked. "Since when? How?" It felt like a bucket of ice water had just been dumped on me. He explained that he had just gotten diagnosed, that it was serious and that he was leaving to Mexico to spend his remaining time in his hometown —plus treatment in America was too expensive, and he didn't have health insurance.

"I'm making a quick stop in Vegas to do a goodbye party before I leave for good," he said finally. "I was hoping you could come." *A party in Vegas?* I thought. The situation seemed suspicious, but he was crying so hard and so publicly that I figured he had to be telling the truth.

When I got home, I called Yesenia to tell her everything that had happened.

"I'm considering helping him pay for treatment so he doesn't have to go back to Mexico without his family," I said.

"I understand," she said. "It's hard to cut ties with someone who was important to you, especially if he just got diagnosed with cancer."

There was a pause for a moment before she continued.

"Listen, I don't want you to feel bad about not being with him in this difficult time, and I don't want to stand between you two if you want to give it another try. Quite honestly, I don't think your ex is actually dying from cancer, because who goes to Vegas for a goodbye party if they're dying? Still, you should probably be there to support him in case it's true. Go back and take care of him. I just can't promise that I'll be here waiting for you."

After our call, I walked in the bathroom and caught my reflection in the mirror. Everything started to hit me at once. I was leaving a business behind, going through a confusing split that was as serious as a divorce, while trying to make sense of these new romantic feelings I had, and now my ex-boyfriend was possibly dying of cancer?

I needed to hear the familiar voice that had always comforted me, so I called my mom.

"Hello, my love," she said—her voice was so warm it almost brought a tear to my eye. "How are you doing?

I knew I couldn't tell my parents that I might be falling in love with a woman, especially because I didn't even know what that meant to me yet. I remembered my dad once telling me how glad he was to have daughters and saying: "*If I had a gay boy, I'd kill him!*" He wasn't being literal, but he *was* incredibly homophobic. Things with my dad were okay now, but if I told him what I was really feeling, I knew Troy would burn again.

Instead of getting too personal, I talked in circles about how overwhelmed I felt and all the stress I was going through from the separation from Alec.

"You know your cousin, Rommy?" she said. "She just went on a 10-day silent meditation retreat." As she explained, Rommy had gone on a vipassana retreat, which was a long mindfulness meditation experience, where you stayed silent the *entire* time.

On some level, it sounded scary and intimidating, but considering how chaotic my life had become, it was also strangely appealing. *Disappearing from the world and not talking to anyone for 10 days is exactly what I need,* I thought.

I pictured myself as Beth, my favorite character from *The L Word*, and how she had gone on a silent retreat while she was going through a separation with Tina. On the show, she had found the peace she needed while walking around a gong and repeating mantras.

After I got off the phone, I decided to search "vipassana retreat" online and see what came up. To my surprise, there was a retreat in Washington happening the very next week! For the first time since the difficult conversation with Yesenia, I felt a glimmer of hope. *Maybe this is exactly what I need,* I thought. *Ten days of complete silence.* If I could quiet my mind and get away from the distractions, maybe I would be able to find the answers to my questions.

After signing up for the retreat, I got an email with the instructions, which I skimmed. Finally, when the day came, I drove out to Onalaska, which was about four hours from Pasco. The retreat was located on six acres of land, surrounded by forest, and all of the guests had their own small cabins with bathrooms attached. The more experienced retreaters were sleeping in tents outside, believing that the discomfort would push them even further beyond their limits, thus heightening their experience. There was also an outbuilding with a kitchen and another domed building that hosted the group meditations. In all, there were about 16 women and men, though each of our groups was kept separate.

Upon arrival, we had to leave our phones at the front office (though even if we kept them on us, we wouldn't have gotten any reception). Everyone who came signed a waiver that they would complete the retreat and wouldn't leave before it concluded, even if they wanted to. As I read the form, one of the bottom lines surprised me:

> By signing this form, you agree not to hold the organizers responsible if completing this retreat results in any negative mental health effects, whether long or short-term.

It was a little scary—the retreat was supposed to help me clear my head and find some peace, not make things worse. I tried to shake any negativity from my mind and signed the form, reminding myself that this was where I needed to be.

After all the paperwork was out of the way, we all got changed into white cotton yogi clothes and sat in the group meditation room where the teachers explained how the days would go during the retreat.

At 5 am, they would ring a gong and wake us up for silent meditation in our room until 6 am. From 6 to 9 am, everyone at the retreat would gather under the giant dome for a group meditation before having breakfast. After breakfast, there were another series of meditations throughout the day with short breaks, then dinner and bedtime, before doing it all over again for a total of 12 hours of silent meditation each day. Finally, all the meals we ate would be vegan to keep our bodies as pure as possible.

The teachers turned on a big screen and showed us videos of our primary teacher, S.N. Goenka, a deceased yogi from

India who now lived on through his recordings. The instructors had already made clear that we weren't allowed to talk to anybody or make physical contact with anyone—not even eye contact—but the recordings expanded on that lesson.

"You must observe the divine silence," S.N. Goenka said in his peaceful voice. I took a deep breath in and released it. It would be difficult to follow all the rules, but I was willing to get out of my comfort zone to find peace.

On day one, the most beautiful thing happened: I woke up to deer outside my cabin eating fruit, and marveled at how in touch with nature I felt. Though my mind was still busy with chatter as I sat down and meditated, I was surprised to find it relatively easy to follow all the rules, even if it was strange to be quiet for so long. On day two, my mind was even louder, and things were a little more difficult. I was thinking about past conversations I'd had and moments when I'd said things I shouldn't have, playing out scenarios in my head of how things would have gone if I'd done X instead of Y. I was getting a little restless, but was still able to focus on the rules, which were simple at first: focus on the breath coming out of my nose and feel it on my upper lip.

Finally, on day three, everything changed. The thoughts in my head had never been louder, and all of them were scrambling to escape. *Oh my God*, I thought. *I need to get out of here!* Still, I remembered the waiver I had signed and knew that I couldn't go back on my word by leaving. There was nothing I could do except sit with the silence (and my internal chaos).

Day four was just as hard as day three, and my internal noise was so loud that I worried I might completely lose my grip on myself. *Just quiet your mind*, I thought. *Stay focused.* The organizers hadn't given us any mantras to repeat to ourselves, but I kept repeating *om* in my head, because otherwise I'd be overwhelmed with my thoughts. I concentrated on how the air I was breathing touched my upper lip, focusing only on that sensation.

Sitting in my yogi clothes in the group meditation dome, I ignored my racing thoughts and instead just focused on my mantra and my breath. Suddenly, something was changing inside me. I began to feel a kind of bubble of energy inside my body that was becoming smaller and smaller. I realized that the bubble was me, which meant that *I* was becoming smaller and smaller inside the physical vessel of my body.

The outside world had disappeared and I was just a tiny speck of energy inside a huge fleshy envelope—my own body. Then, the darkness in front of me started taking different shapes, and I was looking directly at snarling monsters. Everything in my body told me to open my eyes to make the visions stop, but there was also a warm sensation that told me to stay where I was, face to face with my fears.

After a few minutes of staring down these apparitions around me, the monsters began to disappear and everything inside me stopped. On the other side of it, I was in complete bliss and peace. I had no more chatter in my mind; instead, I was in the peaceful "void" that I had heard about before, but never experienced. That sense of peace left shortly after it arrived, but something inside me had changed. *There is something on the other side of all this*, I thought. *What I want is on the other side of this fear, but I have to be brave enough to confront it.*

While the first three days had been difficult, day four felt like a breakthrough. Though we couldn't talk throughout the retreat, we were allowed to ask the instructors for guidance in extreme circumstances and if we had questions. When the meditation was over, I went up to an instructor who wore a turban, had a long mustache styled into two thin, upward-pointing curves like Salvador Dali and exuded peace and serenity. I explained what had happened and asked him what it all meant. He smiled.

"Ah, beautiful," he said. "It sounds like you allowed your soul to cast off its corporeal envelope and let it wander into the darkest corners of your thoughts to confront your own demons. We all have them, but you faced yours. Whatever fear you had in the moment represented itself as monsters. What probably happened is you conquered them and made it to the other side. You were strong enough to do it, and not everybody is—so congratulations!" I smiled. "Now return to your practice and find out what those fears are and how you can conquer them in real life."

From day four onward, I went back and forth between a blissful, spiritual inner state and my noisy thoughts, but the inner peace was getting stronger and stronger as more time passed. Every morning I woke up, greeted the deer outside my cabin and plunged deep into peaceful meditation. Finally, on the 10th day, the instructors began to prepare us for our transition back into the real world. As they warned, it could be quite shocking to the system to go from complete divine silence to trying to explain the same experience to your family members back home.

To help us prepare for the transition, they eased the rules a bit, allowing us to spend a little bit more time talking to the other participants and the instructors. After so much silence, being able to speak again was a complete shock. My voice sounded so loud that my ears hurt to hear it, and all I wanted to do was whisper. In a way, it felt like I was hearing my own voice for the first time—and I couldn't stop thinking about the life-changing experience that had happened on day four.

Before driving home from the retreat, I sat with my thoughts for a few hours. I had gone into Vipassana not knowing what the outcome was going to be, but the confrontation with my inner demons seemed like a signpost. Sitting with it with my eyes closed, I started to interpret it: *I'm afraid of admitting the truth to myself. I'm afraid of coming out and letting go of a relationship I know, which is scary. But if I can move past it, there will be peaceful bliss at the end.*

When I opened my eyes, I took a breath and had a smile on my face. On the way home, I picked up my phone and called Yesenia. After a few rings, she answered.

"Hello?"

"I'm going to come out," I said definitively. "I don't know exactly when or how, but I'll do it in my own time. And I don't have any doubts about us anymore. I'm all in."

Shortly after I got back to the Tri-Cities, I received a call from Alec's life insurance agent. Alec had forgotten that we'd applied together for life insurance a few months prior, and both of us had done physical exams and blood tests. I was still his emergency contact, so the agent called to explain that both of our exams showed that we were healthy, and that our quote would be even cheaper than they initially told us.

"So, Alec is healthy?" I asked, with surprise.

"Very much so," the agent replied. "Congratulations!" *Yesenia was right all along*, I thought. *Alec never even had cancer.* As the news sank in, I couldn't help but laugh a little. Before the retreat, it felt like my world was ending; hearing this news was a relief—both because Alec wasn't going to die, and because now I knew *beyond a doubt* that I'd made the right decision in leaving him.

To celebrate some of the drama being behind us, Yesenia and I went out for a night of drinks and fun to celebrate things finally falling into place. We went to a dance club with live banda—a regional Mexican music—and the dance floor was full of men and women dancing together. There was a huge Mexican community in the Tri-Cities, and the culture tended to be traditional, conservative and masculine—there were lots of macho men with large mustaches and sombreros, who didn't seem like they were particularly supportive of gay identities and lifestyles.

I turned to Yesenia with a big smile and pulled her onto the dance floor, which surprised her. Even though I was barely out of the closet, I didn't care. I had made the choice to be myself, and I had chosen the person I wanted to be with.

This is who I'm going to be, I thought happily while dancing banda with her, *whether people approve of it or not!*

7

HOMECOMING

> *"Under, and back of, the Universe of Time, Space and Change, is ever to be found The Substantial Reality—the Fundamental Truth."*
>
> —THE KYBALION

The afterglow of the retreat had me connecting things in my life that I had never connected before. As a girl, my mother and I had often talked about spirituality, meditation, visualization and inner peace, but over time, I'd lost my grounding to those ideas. Still, with a new perspective, I was ready to start fresh—even if some of the habits I'd learned fell by the wayside pretty quickly.

I tried to continue to meditate, but as I got busier, I ended up stopping the habit completely. I also tried to maintain a vegan diet, until Yesenia and I went to Las Vegas and got hungry in the middle of the night, when the only option available was McDonald's. Initially I ordered apple slices with peanut butter, but Yesenia's dollar cheeseburger smelled so good that I couldn't resist eating most of it—and from there, it was a short road back to eating meat again.

Though Yesenia and I had only officially been together for about a month, it had felt like a year because of the deep connection we had—and because everything in our lives had been moving very fast. She had been living at a house her mom had bought for her and her sister to live in while in college and I was renting my own apartment, but it was inevitable that we would soon move in together (it was like a joke she told me early into our relationship: on a first date, lesbians show up in a U-Haul truck).

Around the same time, Lucio called us with some news that he was getting divorced and had to move out of his house, so we got together for coffee to support him through a difficult transition in his life.

"I think it's for the best," Lucio said sadly. "Even though I tried so hard to make it work, this could be a time to discover some things about myself." I nodded.

"I understand what you mean," I said. I hadn't seen him since the vipassana retreat and making the decision to officially be with Yesenia, so it seemed as good a time as any to tell him the truth. "I actually have something to tell you as well."

At this, Lucio sat up in his chair a little bit. I took a breath.

"After leaving Alec, I also realized something about myself," I said slowly. "I'm a lesbian." His eyes widened. "And Yesenia and I have decided we want to make our relationship public." At this, he almost lost his mind.

"I can't believe it!" he practically shouted, attracting attention from the other people in the cafe. After quieting himself down, he continued. "I'm so happy for all three of us. What better news is there than my two best friends dating each other." As we kept talking, Lucio had an idea.

"What if we all moved in together?" he said suddenly. "My ex is keeping our house, and since I have nowhere else to go, I'm keeping my brother's house so it doesn't go into foreclosure. I can't afford the payments by myself, but what if we all moved in together and split the rent? You have no idea how much of a burden you'd be lifting from me."

Although I was comfortable in my own apartment, the idea of splitting rent three ways to save money and help a friend at the same time seemed like a good idea, so I said yes. Yesenia gave it a little more thought, but after a couple of weeks, she agreed as well.

Though we were thrilled about the new living situation, we weren't entirely truthful with our families about what was happening. Yesenia was out of the closet, but she didn't want to tell everyone that we were living together right away; similarly, I was out of the closet in my own life and to my close friends, but I hadn't told my parents yet. Living a romantic life together was a secret, so our cover story for her parents and mine was that we were just roommates.

Shortly after moving in, and after years of not being able to visit my hometown for various reasons, I was finally in a position to plan a trip to Guadalajara to see my friends and family after nearly seven years.

"That's wonderful!" my mother said over the phone when I told her. After discussing it, we decided I would take a two-week trip to Mexico so that we could all catch up—but I had something else on my mind. I knew I needed to take the next step out of the shadows, and to introduce my parents to Yesenia. Still, I couldn't just blurt it out right away and expect them to accept it. The process had to be gradual, and the Mexico trip seemed like a great opportunity.

"Would it be alright if I brought my friend Yesenia?" I asked. "We're roommates and we've become very close. It would mean a lot to me."

"Of course," my mom replied. "We'd be happy to have her. And we're so excited to see you."

When the time came, Yesenia and I got on a flight back to Guadalajara. Though I was excited to see everyone again, I couldn't stop thinking about what I would say about Yesenia. I wanted my parents to get to know Yesenia as a person first before having to deal with the label of lesbian girlfriend. *If they get to like her first*, I reasoned, *then when I do come out, every- thing will be a lot easier.*

Upon touching down, my dad picked us up at the airport at 5 am and greeted us both with warm hugs.

"I thought that since you're here, Carla," he began, "we could pay a visit to your sister, Sandy." I frowned a little. Sandy and I hadn't talked to each other once in the seven years I had been gone, ever since she had said hurtful things about my mother and me, in the midst of the family chaos that had made me want to leave Guadalajara in the first place. My dad could clearly see the emotions on my face, but he continued.

"I know what you're thinking," he said, "but let's put all of this in the past. It's time to make peace." I was uneasy about the whole thing, but since my dad was already driving towards my sister's house, there wasn't much of a choice in the matter.

All three of us drove over to my half-sister's house at six in the morning and knocked on her door. *It should be quick*, I reminded myself quietly, trying to hide my unease. *It's not a big deal.* Finally, my brother-in-law answered the door and let us in, explaining that Sandy was still asleep but that we could all wait in the living room. After a little while, she came downstairs.

"Dad, it's so early," Sandy said groggily. "What happened?"

"I just picked up your sister from the airport," he replied, "and since we were nearby, she wanted to say hi before heading home." At this, Sandy turned to me and smiled weakly.

"Hi, Carla," she said, giving me an awkward hug. "It's been a long time."

"This is my friend, Yesenia," I replied after we separated. Sandy turned to Yesenia and waved, before offering her hand for a handshake.

"Great to meet you," Yesenia said brightly. Sandy smiled back, her eyes lingering on Yesenia for a few moments too long. We all sat down on her couch and talked about life, work and what we had been up to for the past seven years.

"Do you see Carla?" my dad asked Sandy. "Do you see how thin she is now? Remember when you were at that age?" My dad had always made comments like that. Though he never had bad intentions, I knew it was the exact kind of thing that created rivalries between all his daughters.

"Yes, Dad," Sandy replied, rolling her eyes and barely containing the frustration in her voice. "I remember when I was that thin." Nobody said anything too dramatic while we all caught up, but I couldn't help but notice Sandy looking at Yesenia and me, which made me nervous. Finally, my dad spoke up.

"This has been a great visit," he said, "but part of the reason we're here is to put things in the past." With that, he turned to me, expecting me to say something. Internally, I groaned—but instead, I took a breath and started to speak.

"I'm actually getting together with a bunch of friends later this afternoon," I started awkwardly. "Adriana and Raquel are coming and you should come, too."

"Sure," she said politely. "I'd love to come." Though we hadn't made peace about the past, exchanging that invitation felt like it was as close as we were going to get. With the family business officially handled (in my dad's eyes), we were ready to go home again. Later that afternoon, Yesenia and I went to meet our friends at our hotel and sure enough, all three of my sisters came. *Thank God that's over*, I thought. Though our initial reconciliation had been uncomfortable, spending the day at the hotel pool was fun, and I still felt a sense of relief.

For the rest of the two weeks, my parents, Yesenia and I took in sights around Guadalajara and Puerto Vallarta, ate at our favorite restaurants and got to know one another. Yesenia was so outgoing and comfortable with my family right away, and seemed to be winning the approval of both my mom and dad. My mom and I were getting along great as always, and even my dad and I seemed to be past whatever negativity had happened between us.

I was full of hope, which scared me a little. *Maybe I will actually be able to tell them the full truth*, I thought. I knew my mom would accept me and my decisions (as I'd made hints in some of our private conversations), but I wasn't sure my dad would. On top of that, I didn't want to put her in an uncomfortable position by having him find out that she already knew and I hadn't told him, so I wanted to tell them both at the same time.

Every time I tried to bring up the subject, the words got caught in my throat. Finally, the last day of the trip came, and our plan was to go to a family friend's bachelorette party before parting ways. Before the party started, we all went to see my friend perform samba at a Brazilian restaurant. We all ordered caipirinhas—a strong Brazilian cocktail—and got tipsy.

Later, we got in the car and my dad drove us to the bachelorette party, though once we got there, our family friends turned him away at the door. "This party is for girls only," they said with mischievous smiles. "Some of the boys are hanging out outside down the street, so you can go spend time with them!" The two boys were a couple of our gay friends whom we had invited while we were tipsy earlier in the day, and they were at a bar nearby. Hearing all this, my dad was a little disappointed but seemed to understand. With that, he dropped us off and went to park the car.

The energy of the day was a continuation of the celebration we'd had earlier, and my mom, Yesenia and I kept drinking together until the room was blurring slightly at the edges and we were all beginning to get a little emotional. Though I'd been holding back on telling the full truth the entire trip, I knew that the do-or-die moment was approaching quickly.

Yesenia went to get us more drinks and was intercepted by some other friends at the party. Ever since they found out I was dating a girl, they were all excited to meet her. Alone with my mom, I saw the opportunity. *This is it,* I thought. *This is the moment.*

"Mom, I have to tell you something," I mumbled quickly, turning so that we were directly facing each other.

"What is it, my dear?" she replied. I swallowed before continuing.

"Yesenia isn't my friend," I began. "She's my girlfriend. And I think I'm gay." As soon as the words were out of my mouth, I started crying.

"Carlita, it's okay," she said. "I accept you and love you the way you are. And I think I kind of knew already, anyway. When you were a girl, you always wanted to dress like a boy— and you hated dresses!" As I felt relief crash through me, I hugged my mom and cried harder. After the moment passed, I went to find Yesenia and explained what had happened.

All three of us embraced, hugging and kissing one another on the cheeks and enjoying the beautiful moment, until I heard a voice from across the room.

"Carla!" someone yelled. "I think your dad is getting into a fight with someone outside!" *Oh no*, I thought, suddenly wide awake and alert. All three of us got up to walk outside the party, where we found my dad arguing with our two gay friends, who were a couple. As we ran up, our two friends were shoving each other and throwing punches, until they finally broke apart.

"What happened?" my mom demanded.

"Just get in the car," my dad growled. He was fuming, but he wouldn't explain anything. Without any context, we all climbed in and my dad announced he was taking us to the airport, even though it was five hours early. We rode in steely silence for the first half of the drive, until my dad finally spoke.

"This is why I hate faggots so much," he shouted. "They're always making a scene. They all deserve to die!" My stomach dropped, both at his words and because he was talking about my friends. The anger was making my dad drive the car more sharply, causing Yesenia and I to bump into each other in the backseat. Seeing us in the rearview seemed to only make him angrier. "And why do you two have to sit so close together?"

He launched into blaming me for causing the fight to happen and I was suddenly full of anger again, just like when I was a teenager. I could feel words forming in my mouth, and they came out before I could control myself.

"Well, you know what Dad?" I began, but before I could finish my sentence, my mom waved her hand and interrupted me.

"Please, Carlita!" she said urgently. "This is not the moment." Clearly, she knew what words were probably going to come next: *I'm a faggot, too...*

When we got to the airport, my mom hugged us goodbye but my dad was still furious. Before our plane took off, I was scrolling on my phone when I realized what had happened.

While we were at the party, my sister Sandy sent my dad

several screenshots from a Facebook profile that appeared to be Yesenia's. Underneath the pictures were captions:

This is my girlfriend and I want to marry her! <3

Me and the love of my life!

I love you Carla! So glad we are together!

My stomach dropped. I knew that Yesenia had posted those pictures online months ago and tagged me, but those weren't the original captions. After all, she had agreed to let me come out in my own time; these captions were essentially dragging me out of the closet.

"Why would you do this?" I said, showing Yesenia the phone.

"I didn't do that!" she replied. "That's not my profile." She showed me her phone and it was true; the captions weren't the same as the ones she posted originally. After searching on Facebook together, we realized she had two profiles: one that was actually hers, and one that was clearly a fake.

Most of the information on the fake one was barely filled out and there were almost no posts on the timeline. However, there were a bunch of photos of Yesenia and I being close. The entire thing had only been created just days before, and the profile only had five friends—two of whom were my sister Sandy and my dad.

All in a flash, I realized what had happened. My sister had known something was happening between us when we visited her house. To spite me, she must've stolen the pictures from Yesenia, made the fake profile and shown it to my dad.

Now, I saw why he was so angry. He had to process that I was gay—but what was even worse was that I didn't tell him.

Finally, I had lied about who Yesenia was, which I knew he considered a betrayal.

I thought the worst of my relationship with my dad was behind me. Unfortunately, now I realized that the pain was only beginning once again.

8

CAUSE AND EFFECT

"Every Cause has its Effect; every Effect has its Cause; everything happens according to Law; Chance is but a name for Law not recognized."

—*THE KYBALION*

Upon returning, it was clear that the visit had changed things. Having distance from my father had helped before, but now I was constantly getting angry phone calls, texts and emails from him saying terrible things about my mom and me, sometimes about my choices and sometimes about how he thought we had conspired behind his back.

I confessed to my dad that it was true that Yesenia was my girlfriend, even though the Facebook posts hadn't been from us. I didn't want him to think that I came out to the world before I came out to him, which is what hurt him the most. He couldn't understand why I hadn't opened up to him, but it was the simple result of cause and effect. Lying to him didn't make me happy, but I had been subconsciously conditioned to not tell him the truth about this issue. Because of his behavior over the years, I was afraid of him.

Though my mom was calling me whenever she could to give me encouragement, my dad was becoming my enemy. The situation got so bad that I had to start ignoring his calls, but I knew from my mom that things between her and my dad had become more tense than ever.

Despite everything, I was glad that Yesenia had met my mom and that they had gotten along so well—and that there were no more lies to maintain. Most of the people I had talked to who came out of the closet said that it felt like a weight had been lifted, though that wasn't quite how I felt. I felt more pressure than ever, but at least I had Yesenia to make everything feel better.

Living together was giving us more of an opportunity to deepen our relationship, but it was unusual because we had a roommate. Although things had started off well with Lucio, our relationship was starting to become a bit suffocating.

Shortly after we were back from Mexico, one of Lucio's friends came to the house with a bag full of my clothes.

"I wanted to return these," she said, handing me the bag. "I was here with Lucio the other day and he convinced me to go out dancing with him. I didn't have any clothes, but he said I could go in your closet and borrow whatever. Thanks so much!" I stood there baffled as she handed me the clothes and started to walk away.

"Your car is so nice by the way," she added. "Thanks for letting us borrow it!" I had left my keys at the house while I was out of town, but I'd never said anyone could borrow my car.

One Sunday morning, Yesenia and I were lying together in our bed watching a movie when the door to our bedroom burst open and Lucio came running in, jumping into bed with us.

"Good morning, besties," he said, snuggling up to both of us. "What are we doing today?" Though he wasn't interrupting anything too serious, Yesenia and I were both in our room with the door closed for a reason—and although he was our best friend, we were *not* comfortable with him jumping into bed with us.

"Lucio, can you give us a minute?" I asked. "We're watching a movie and we're not dressed." He stared at me for a second before rolling his eyes.

"Oh my gosh," he said. "Relax. You're under the covers and I can't see anything—plus I don't even want to see you anyway." Even though we were clearly uncomfortable, he still didn't leave and kept watching a movie with us until he finally got bored and left. Once he was gone, Yesenia turned to me with a wry expression.

"Maybe it's time to discuss getting our own place together," she said. "What do you think?" Though it had always been a goal of ours to live together exclusively, the need for our living situation was changing more rapidly than we expected.

I was excited at the idea of getting a house with Yesenia, but it still seemed like a far-fetched dream. I had inquired before about what it would cost to buy a home in Pasco, and buying a $200,000 home would mean putting 20 percent down, at least according to what I'd been told at the time—as the lender claimed we wouldn't qualify for a zero-down program or a 3.5 percent FHA loan. Hearing that had made it seem so unreachable, so I let the idea go.

Since I had officially ended things with Alec, I had left our bar business behind entirely and was focused only on Language Spot, so I had lost part of my income. Even though I was making good money from my interpreting business, I had never had a good handle on my budget and spending. Fortunately, Yesenia had always had good habits with money, and she had actually already saved the amount we needed.

Though my family had been comfortable in Mexico when I was a child, Yesenia's childhood in Mexico had been humble. Her mom became an orphan at age five and learned to work shortly after, selling sour cream and tamales from door to door. She became a merchant at a young age, and coming to the US without speaking English didn't stop her.

As she got older, she learned how to purchase vacant lots and mobile homes at auctions, reselling them later for a profit, after fixing them or placing a mobile home on the lots. Though she lived in a humble mobile home in Mattawa, Washington herself, her passive income was high and she was incredibly thrifty when it came to spending it. As a result, she had saved money and was comfortable, financially speaking. Her success in America was inspiring, and her mindset had clearly rubbed off on Yesenia as she was growing up.

After consulting Yesenia's mom that purchasing a house would be a better investment than renting (especially given how housing prices were going up), Yesenia and I started searching for houses together. After touring a few houses with a real estate agent, we decided that we wanted a new construction home, so we could pick our colors and make it our own. Eventually, we signed a contract on a house in Pasco. After six more months of living with Lucio, Yesenia and I moved in together on our own.

Since money was tight between moving costs and getting settled in a new house, Yesenia and I were determined to grow financially to make life more comfortable again. To grow my business even more, I thought of getting another set of certifications to expand. Though medical interpretation had been going well, I knew that court interpreting would be even more lucrative. Still, I knew the exam was a difficult one. At our house-warming party, Yesenia and I discussed our court interpreting idea with Lucio, since we'd heard him mention it in the past as well, and we all signed up to take the exam.

"I just bought a few of the books for the court exam," I told him. "Some of them are expensive, but since I'm not going to read them all at once I can share them with you. Maybe if you get other books, we can all share notes?" Lucio nodded quietly as if he wanted to say something. A moment later, he shook his glass of ice to show that he had finished his drink.

"Baby, pour me another tequila, please," he said. Confused, I took the glass from him and refilled it. I wasn't sure if he was becoming more selfish or if I just hadn't noticed his behavior before, but it was frustrating; Yesenia was noticing it as well.

Since we didn't live together anymore, Lucio could no longer jump into bed with us. Instead, he would show up unannounced at our house.

"I came over because I need a drink," he would simply say, letting himself in and going through our cabinets to see what bottles we had. While Yesenia and I had liked to party for a while, we were settling in together as a couple, and watching movies at home on a Saturday night felt better than going out. I could see that Lucio felt like he was potentially losing two friends at once, but we couldn't keep up with his constant partying and drinking anymore (and didn't want to). Now, we needed our own space.

About three weeks later, I ran into a medical interpreter at the hospital who had just passed his court interpreter test and told him I was studying. His eyes lit up.

"I have the best thing for you," he said. "I have a glossary of all the terms you need to know for the exam that I relied on when I took it. It's basically a cheat sheet, and if you study it, you'll pass!" Considering how dense all the material I'd already been looking at was, I was so excited that there might be another, easier way to prepare.

"That's so great, thank you," I replied. "Can you send it to me via email?" After that, we exchanged information and sure enough, he sent the cheat sheet through. Right away, I copied the email to Lucio and added a kind message to it:

> Guess what? We just got the cheat sheet to pass the exam! Enjoy :)

After I sent the email, I got another one back from him a few minutes later:

> Ha, this is great but I already have this—the same inter-preter sent it to me a few weeks ago. I thought you would've noticed my email address on the thread?

After hearing this, Yesenia and I were both confused and upset. If he already had all the material that we needed to study, why wouldn't he have just shared it with us? Particularly when I had offered to share course books with him just a few weeks earlier? The next time we saw him, we decided to ask him about it in person.

"I don't understand," I began. "I thought we agreed that we were going to work together and help each other study for this exam."

"Why didn't you tell us you had all this when we talked about it?" Yesenia asked. "This is way better than all the books we bought!"

"I don't have to share everything that I study," he said. In a sense, he was right; he wasn't obligated to share anything with us. But we were supposed to be friends, and we had agreed to help each other. I couldn't understand why he would've purposely hid information from us that would've made our lives easier. "Besides," he continued, "what have you done for me to request that I do something like that for you in exchange?"

"We have all done a lot to help each other, because that's what friends do," Yesenia said. "It was a bit upsetting to learn that you didn't share the list, but it's even more upsetting to hear that you purposely didn't share it because we didn't do something for you first."

"Calm down," Lucio said dismissively. "You're both over-reacting."

What Yesenia had said was true. Both of us had helped Lucio plenty of times. Throughout his divorce, we had paid his rent for several months in advance, I had given him work through my agency and Yesenia had also let him work in her office on some weekends, keeping whatever profits he made.

After our conversation, Yesenia and I knew we had to start putting up more firm boundaries with Lucio. Whatever limited collaboration we had for studying ended, and we finished preparing for the exam separately from that point on, even though I was still assigning Lucio interpreting appointments.

"I think it's important to keep friendship and business separate," I explained to Yesenia when she asked me about it. "But after all, it's thanks to him that I have an agency in the first place, and I know he could use the extra money." Yesenia nodded, but she looked a little uneasy.

"Just be careful," she said finally. "I don't have a good feeling about him anymore."

When the time finally came, Yesenia and I both took the court interpreting exam, and Lucio never showed up. As promised, the test was incredibly difficult—even with all the time and energy we'd poured into preparing for it. When it was all over, we got an email announcing that our results were viewable, and were bitterly disappointed: neither one of us had passed.

"I don't know what to do now," I said to Yesenia. "Business is going well, but I don't know if I want to do medical interpreting for my entire life." She listened to me, rubbing my back.

"I understand you're disappointed, but maybe you're looking at this the wrong way," she said. "What you probably want is a change, and I can understand that. What about going back to school?" I hesitated.

"I don't know," I began—but she cut me off.

"Listen," she said, "whatever you think about not being able to do it or not being good enough has to stop now. Forget whatever Alec said in the past—I *know* you're smart and can achieve whatever you want to. Plus, look at where he's at now!"

It was true; Alec hadn't fared well after we'd separated. Though I'd agreed to give him control of the bar that we'd started together, he had run the business into the ground in six months and had lost it. Since then, he had fallen off the map. Even though Alec had torn down my confidence in the past, it made me sad to hear that the bar was closing.

After my conversation with Yesenia, I kept thinking about Dr. Leenards, who was still my favorite client. In his house, you could see his intelligence all over the place from all his degrees hanging on the wall. His energy was always so warm and inviting, and whenever he caught me looking at one of his degrees, he would make it known that he thought I should go back to school too.

Finally, I decided I would do it. Maybe going back to school was the change I needed. Still, I had no idea what I wanted to study. Knowing I had to pick something, my first thought was that I would study linguistics. I had heard that the FBI hired interpreters with linguistics degrees to do interesting, secret work, and it seemed as good a place to apply my skills as any other.

To get into community college, I took an admissions test and though I hadn't been in a classroom in nearly seven years, I still scored at college level in all subjects except for math. Hearing my results, Yesenia was surprised.

"Babe," she said, "I knew you were smart, but I think you're even smarter than I thought—maybe even smarter than *you* thought!" It was true, the results had surprised me after feeling discouraged for so long. With Yesenia's constant encouragement to think more highly of myself and be more confident in my opinions, I started attending community college and working towards an associate's degree.

As I pondered what I might study, I thought more about Dr. Leenards. Spending time with him had made me think about becoming a psychologist myself, though I also knew that would mean seven years of school. I still wasn't positive where I would end up, but I knew I didn't have to decide right away. *Nothing is set in stone yet*, I thought. *At the very least, I can get the base-level courses out of the way first.*

Soon after I started college, I got a call from my mom, who was in tears.

"Carla," she said between heavy breaths. "Things with your dad are not good. I caught him cheating with the *sirvienta*, and when I asked him for an explanation, he became furious and violent." Hearing this, my heart was racing. "We were in the back office of the salon and he pushed me to the sofa, but I managed to get away from him. I've decided that I'm leaving your dad for good."

"Wait, what?" I asked. "Are you okay? Where will you go?"

"I'm okay," she continued. "I'm safe in Rosy's house with Carmelita. She overheard everything and helped me get out of the salon." My heart warmed at the mention of Rosy, remembering how she had helped me escape harm from my dad seven years prior, and for Carmelita, who had been working with my mom since before I was even born.

"I'm going to stay here until your dad calms down," my mom continued, "until we can have a serious and definite conversation about divorce."

"Mom, Yesenia and I have our own house here in the Tri-Cities," I said suddenly. "If you want to come here while things settle down with dad, you are more than welcome to."

Upon hearing this, my mom cried and cried even harder. Though she tried to object, saying that it was too much of an inconvenience, I insisted. Though we hadn't decided anything, she appreciated the offer and we ended our conversation. She called me back several days later, crying again.

"Carlita, your dad is not being cooperative with the separation," she said. "I don't know what to do." As she explained, my father was not letting her take any money with her and had already cut her out of shared bank accounts and shared assets. If she was going to leave him, she was going to have to leave with nothing—only a few hundred dollars and a suitcase full of clothes.

"Mom, you always know what to do," I said. "Do what you always tell me to do: follow your gut." After thinking it over for a moment, she finally replied.

"My peace of mind is worth more than any amount in the bank," she said sadly. "Your dad can keep the money if that makes him happy. If the offer to stay with you is still open, I'd like to take it—thankfully I can still work, so I'll get back on my feet and start helping with rent."

My heart hurt hearing what my mom was saying. She was 64—an age when most people were thinking about retirement—and she had been working since she was a teenager. Still, instead of feeling bad for herself, she was grateful that she could still work.

"You can stay with us for as long as you want," I replied. "We will help you in any way that we can—don't worry about the money."

I was extremely disappointed in my dad's attitude. I had remembered conversations about my parents sharing all of their assets and finances, but my dad had always said it was only out of convenience and nothing more. *If you ever left me*, I could hear him saying to my mom in some barely remembered memory, *we would easily split everything up, 50-50, no questions asked. For now, having everything in one place is best for convenience.*

Of course, after hearing what our plan was, my father immediately started texting and calling more intensely than he'd ever done before—and his messages were nastier than they had ever been. In the middle of class, I was constantly getting messages from my dad:

As usual, you are being the apple of discord.

What you're doing is separating your parents—just like you always wanted.

You nasty lesbians will pay for this! Everything will come back to you three times worse!

Every time I read one of them, adrenaline ran through my entire body. Each one triggered my fear and panic, reminding me of the most violent episodes I had ever had with my dad. Even so, I couldn't help myself from replying to him angrily whenever I saw one:

Dad, mom says she left you because you cheated on her.
What does me being a lesbian have to do with that?

He replied:

You're both being brainwashed by that woman you are
so infatuated with. Your mom told me that she doesn't
even like her.

I knew my dad too well to believe him; he just wanted to start conflict between us any way he could. Throughout the situation, Yesenia saw everything that was happening and was very supportive the entire time. Even though living with her mother-in-law wasn't an ideal situation, she was more than open to it, and seeing her big heart on display only made me love her even more.

Over time, my dad was getting angrier and angrier that I was stealing his wife from him—and he was doing everything he could to hurt me as a way of getting revenge. All I wanted to do was focus on the next chapter of my life, but instead I was getting trapped in another vicious and toxic relationship. My dad was bombarding me with negative energy to hold me down, and as much as I would try to keep it away, it crept up and dragged me down.

I felt like a bird trying to fly out of a briar patch, who was constantly running into branches, bleeding and falling back down again. I was hitting an emotional rock bottom and didn't know what to do until I sat down with Yesenia to discuss everything.

"I know it's painful that you don't have his support," she said. "But sometimes we keep these relationships going and don't cut strings, even when we need to for our own health. Is he adding to your life or subtracting from it?"

I thought about it. Of course, I was so grateful for everything he did for me as a child. Thanks to him and the fact that I was bilingual, I had a nice-paying job and a good life. I was very grateful, and I knew that he loved me.

"Vampires do exist," Yesenia added. "Vampires of energy. Some people add energy, some people are neutral and others subtract it." In that moment, it was hard to deny that he was subtracting more than he was adding, as painful as that was. I needed to be in a good state of mind if I was going to succeed, get good grades and have a chance of transferring to a reputable university.

"You deserve to be surrounded by people who love you the way *you* want to be loved, not the way they *choose* to show you love," she continued. "I'm sure your dad loves you, but if he doesn't love you the way *you* want to be loved, sometimes it's okay to create distance if people are not respecting your boundaries."

Her words were making so much sense. Though I often felt guilty about ignoring my dad or temporarily blocking him, every time we communicated, we both ended up even angrier and more agitated. It was a vicious cycle that neither of us could stop. Still, for some reason, Yesenia's words were putting things into perspective.

As I looked at the relationship Yesenia and I had together, I realized that I felt safe, respected and encouraged to be the best version of myself possible. Whenever I asked for love and care the way I wanted it, she was ready and willing to give it to me, and vice versa, and I was still not used to it. *There's nothing I can do to control my anger*, I could hear my dad saying after his outbursts in the past.

It's in my family's blood, running through my veins, he would say. *This is who I am!*

"No," I'd reply, "*it's the way you've* been *in the past. It doesn't mean you have to continue to be like that.*"

A tree that grows askew will never have a straight trunk, he would reply, a common Mexican saying that he would quote to defend himself with.

I realized that I had to create distance with him again and cut our emotional ties because he wasn't going to change. I told myself that he would still have a place in my heart, but energetically, he would no longer have any control over me; I couldn't let his judgments or words affect my decisions and what I knew I had to do.

As before, it was difficult to cut ties with my dad. We both fueled each other's anger, and at times it felt like a drug that I was addicted to. Even so, I knew I had to quit for my own good and for my sanity. But the worst part was how badly I felt for my mom.

Although I thought I could handle whatever emotional issues were between my father and me directly, what was happening between my mom and him was taking me to a dark place. *What if it is really my fault that my parents are separating? Should I be encouraging my mom to fix things with dad instead?*

When the day came that my mom showed up on our doorstep, the tears were unavoidable. As we hugged and I welcomed her in, I felt words coming up that I couldn't control.

"I'm so sorry, Mom," I said, crying. "I feel like I caused all this. If I had just said less or been different, maybe none of this would have happened." At that, my mom wiped my tears away and told me to shush.

"No, Carlita, it's not your fault at all," she replied. "Everything happens for a reason; nothing happens by chance. This is exactly where we both need to be."

9

EBB AND FLOW

"Everything flows out and in; everything has its tides; all things rise and fall; the pendulum-swing manifests in everything; the measure of the swing to the right, is the measure of the swing to the left; rhythm compensates."

—THE KYBALION

With my mom safe, Yesenia and I were determined to get her set up again in America. Early on, Yesenia got my mom a job working at Yesenia's tax office, and things were quiet for about six months. Unfortunately, the day after my mom's six-month tourist visa expired, we got a call from my dad on Yesenia's office line—the only number that wasn't blocked.

"Yesenia," the receptionist told her nervously. "There's a message for you on the answering machine." The message my dad left was an angry one:

"I am just calling to warn you that I am calling immigration on you and your mother, and I'm telling them that Yesenia is a *pollera!*"

It was painful and embarrassing to listen to. Calling Yesenia *pollera* was a serious accusation that, of course, wasn't true—it meant that she was a smuggler or a human trafficker, someone who brings people across the border into the US.

We weren't sure how, but he'd found out where my mom was working. What he didn't know, however, was that my mom had already legalized her permanent resident status through my brother, who'd had been born in the US and with whom we'd reconnected through the internet many years back. While I was happy to have my mom by my side, the situation with my dad felt like a nightmare.

Though my mom had initially blocked my dad to avoid his harassment, she had to unblock him as they went through their divorce paperwork together with their attorneys. It meant that every day, we were getting cruel messages and repeated phone calls from him. I had decided that I wouldn't let my dad have any emotional influence over my life anymore, but every time my mom would get a call from him, my stomach would turn. Still, I knew it was taking even more of a toll on my mom.

Because they'd been married in Guadalajara, my mom had to fly back to Mexico to appear in court—and often my dad would intentionally set court dates, only to not show up. On one occasion, he waited for her in the parking lot, after she'd shown up alone.

"Oh, am I late?" he asked, unapologetically. "I told you before that if you want to divorce me, you won't be taking anything with you. Between me not coming to court and you spending money on tickets from Seattle, we'll see how long you can keep this up."

To complicate things, my dad accused my mom of bigamy. As it turned out, she had never been able to divorce her first husband because he had disappeared before I was born. Ten years later, she decided to put the past behind her and marry my dad. Unfortunately, my dad's strategy worked, and my mom was found guilty of bigamy, and as a result, the judge ruled that my dad would keep all of the marital assets.

The day that everything was decided, my dad called my mom to discuss the results.

"I could still sell everything and we could split it all, 50-50," my dad said. "But only if you come back to Mexico so we can do all the arrangements in person." After hearing that, my mom's decision to stay away from him was more firm than ever.

"Carlita, I used to love your dad very much," she said. "Nobody ever made me feel the way he did at first. But I started to lose respect for him when he began to be violent towards you. It reminded me of my dad, and I don't think I ever forgave him." After a moment, she continued with a lump in her throat and lips quivering. "And the fact that he doesn't feel any remorse for keeping everything, despite how hard I worked all these years, makes me want to never hear from him again."

Though my mom had lived a comfortable and prosperous life in Guadalajara, she was starting over from scratch in the US and needed a way to make money. After brainstorming, the best idea we came up with was to have her start another salon in Pasco, with our help. She already had plenty of experience running her own business back home, and I had experience running a business in the US. Plus, helping her get on her feet again would be a way of giving back to her and supporting her for all the love she'd given me over the years.

First, we needed to find a space to rent. By happenstance, Yesenia's business had had a great year, and she'd been able to save money. As a result, she'd recently put a down payment on the building her office was located in, which had once been a mid-sized health clinic. We had been planning to renovate it and find two tenants for it already, when we realized that one of the spaces would be perfect for my mom's business.

After borrowing money from Yesenia's parents for the renovations, we started visualizing how the space might look and explained to the contractors what we were looking for. With a small team in place, we renovated the two suites within a few months, and I used my credit cards to buy my mom all the furniture she would need for the salon. With everything in place, we moved my mom into her new space as our first tenant.

The entire time we were doing renovations, I was attending classes at community college and realizing how much I loved to learn. Though I had always had good grades in school, my focus had been more on the social aspects. This time, it was different. I wanted to spend all my time with Yesenia and my mom, so I skipped socializing, focused on my grades and found myself fascinated by literature, philosophy and psychology. I was realizing that I would soon have to think about choosing a major and transferring to a bigger university.

"Let me take you on a tour of the University of Washington," Yesenia said excitedly one day. "Maybe you'll fall in love with it like I did. I bet you would love living in the big city." After talking it over, we decided to take a weekend trip to Seattle.

As soon as we were on campus, I saw that Yesenia had been right. I had never seen such beautiful cherry blossom trees, which was one of the university's main attractions in the spring, and I loved seeing all the college students gathered on the quad, studying together. She took me through the Suzzallo Library, which had enormously tall ceilings, stained glass windows and lots of natural light. It looked exactly like the Great Hall of Hogwarts from the Harry Potter movies, and I was instantly in love.

"This place is amazing," I told Yesenia, "but do you really think I can get in?"

"Of course," she said. "You are so smart and dedicated. I know you'll get in if you apply yourself." As ever, I loved how much she encouraged me, and her love was helping me regain whatever confidence I'd lost.

Heeding her advice, I tried as hard as I could in school and stayed on the honor roll every quarter. As time passed, my dream of going to the University of Washington seemed more and more possible.

"Since you like to say that you attract things through visualization and being in a good state of mind," Yesenia said to me after a few more months, "let's go to Seattle again to look at neighborhoods we'd want to live in if you get accepted—sorry, *when* you get accepted."

We planned another weekend trip and did a tour of a handful of open houses. Though we didn't see any that we were in love with, we were getting an idea of prices. On our last tour of the day, we decided to look at a block of condos.

"Babe, I think we're really going to like these condos," Yesenia said, based on what she'd seen on the internet, "but since we're just looking and not buying anything, let's not mislead the agent." I nodded in agreement and we began the condo tour. Of all the places we saw that day, the condos were by far our favorite.

Everything was new construction, and though they were priced the same as the townhouses we'd seen, they came with a lot more amenities—including an open rooftop on the 41st floor! As the agent told us, the condos would be ready in two years, which was perfect timing for if I got accepted. *When I get accepted*, I corrected myself.

"Plus," the agent added, "there's a rumor going around that Amazon might build their headquarters directly across from us.

Once that knowledge goes public, the prices are going to skyrocket."

"What are the requirements to hold a spot?" Yesenia asked.

"You just need five percent of the purchase price in earnest money," the agent replied. "The remaining down payment will be due when the condo is ready and you sign the closing documents in two years." Upon hearing this, Yesenia turned to me.

"Do you like it?" she asked, smiling widely with her eyebrows raised.

"I love it," I said, smiling back, "but I haven't even applied yet!" I was very intrigued about what she was about to suggest.

"I have enough for earnest money but not for the down payment," Yesenia began. "We have two years to work our butts off—two tax seasons to save money and make it work. I know we can, but we have to be on the same channel if you really want to do this." Before she had even finished the sentence, I had already said yes.

As Yesenia explained, living in a condo in Seattle had been a dream of hers for a long time. Now that it aligned with my dreams, we both wanted to jump in immediately. Of course, we would have to be strategic, or we would lose our deposit, which was around $25,000. After making that decision, we were more determined than ever to focus on our goals—which sometimes meant Yesenia calling attention to some of my financial habits.

"Babe, has anyone told you that you're a bit of a shopaholic?" she asked, with a smile on her face while we were at an outlet store. I stopped in my tracks, putting the bag I was holding back down. I felt immediately embarrassed.

"What do you mean?" I demanded. She shrugged and smiled.

"That's the reason why I work! So I can spend money on things I like and enjoy," I replied, a little irritated.

"I know we're comfortable," she said, "but with these new

expenses, we should think more about saving. Especially if we're going to get a condo in Seattle."

What she said made sense. Deep down, I knew Yesenia was right about my spending habits; it was a conversation we'd had many times before. In my previous relationship, I had always spent all of my money because I hadn't had a clear plan for the future. I had never had a "why" in place before, but now that was changing.

Yesenia and I wanted to have a financially stable future together, beginning with moving into this condo. It was a shared "why," which shed some light on things that would need to change. With my mom by my side and Yesenia's encouragement, I finally had a reason to develop better financial habits. Because of that, I was determined to run my agency even more efficiently than I had before and to find more interpreters, so I could grow.

I kept giving Lucio appointments for a while, even though we were no longer spending time together as friends. On some level, I didn't have the courage to stop giving him appointments since it was thanks to him that I had started my business in the first place—and since I had so many appointments to cover, I knew I could still use him.

Though he had reached out to Yesenia and me to try to repair things, we realized that we didn't want a friend who had such a transactional view of relationships. I had initially thought that we might be able to keep our work and personal lives separate, but soon I was feeling the strain in my business as well.

I had given Lucio a week's worth of appointments and at the last second, he canceled and said he wouldn't be available for any of them because he had a trip to Vegas that had just come up.

"Lucio, come on," I said in frustration. "I gave you these

appointments weeks ago! I could have assigned them to someone else, but it's going to be hard to find a replacement now with no advance notice!"

"Sorry," he said simply. "You'll find a way to figure it out." Most of my interpreters got their appointments at least a week in advance, and finding someone to cover last-minute appointments was not always easy. Since I already filled a lot of appointments myself, if someone canceled at the last minute, I often had to give appointments away to other agencies and lose out on the money.

It wasn't the first time Lucio had done something like this, but I was determined that it would be the last.

"Lucio, I understand," I said. "But please also understand that I can't continue to assign you appointments anymore. This is not the first time you've left me hanging with assigned appointments because you have to meet a friend or 'something came up.' I need someone who is more reliable."

"Do as you wish," he replied. A few days later, he sent me a text:

Carla, I know I offered to be your immigration sponsor, but I need you to take me off your paperwork.

I had been a permanent resident for several years, and part of keeping that status meant having a sponsor who would be responsible for repaying the United States if I ever received any means-tested public benefits, like food stamps or Medicaid, though I hadn't used any in the nine years I'd lived in America. Though Lucio had said it would be an honor to sponsor me two years prior when we were roommates and best friends, I wasn't surprised that he no longer wanted that responsibility. I sent a simple text in response:

No problem.

I figured it would be fine to use Yesenia as my sponsor instead, until my immigration attorney reached out to me with a warning.

"It's not as simple as just switching your sponsor," she said. "It can't be done all that easily. When someone signs an affidavit of support, they become legally and financially responsible for their sponsored immigrant until that person becomes a US citizen or gets credited with 40 quarters of work."

After getting off the phone with her, I texted Lucio back.

"I'm sorry, but my attorney says I can't take you off my application until I become a citizen," I said. "It should happen in less than one year, but there's nothing I can do until then."

"Find a way," he replied coldly. Frustrated, I went to the Department of Homeland Security's website, found a paragraph and pasted it to him directly as a text message to show him there was no way I could end his sponsorship until I became a citizen:

> *Your obligation as a sponsor ends if you or the individual sponsored dies or if the individual sponsored ceases to be a lawful permanent resident and departs the United States.*

After a moment, he replied:

See? There IS a way.

I didn't bother responding, and it was the last text message Lucio ever sent me.

As I finished my associate's degree with a 3.86 GPA, I was ready to apply to UW with what I thought was a strong application. As I sent it in, I was pleased to find myself more confident than I thought I'd be and couldn't wait to hear back. Though I had to apply to general admissions first, my plan was to later apply directly to the psychology department to keep exploring my interest in the brain and human behavior, inspired by my work with Dr. Leenards.

I loved my interpreting sessions with him because of how he blended Eastern medicine and ancient wisdom with his own holistic, spiritual approach. Plus, I had taken enough classes at school to learn that some mental health practitioners were beginning to explore more unorthodox methods to treat patients, such as using LSD and psilocybin in their therapy sessions.

For some reason, I felt very drawn to the idea of treating illness with hallucinogenic and ancestral medicines in order to create a spiritual transformation. After months of waiting, I finally got my acceptance letter. Everything we had envisioned was coming true: I was going to attend UW, and Yesenia and I were going to move to Seattle. Still, I knew I had a lot of work to do to prepare for our move. For a long time, Lucio had been my right-hand man at The Language Spot, covering most of the appointments for me. To replace him, I needed to find more interpreters to make up the shortfall—particularly because I wanted to have enough money for both our move and school.

To fix the issue, I worked on recruiting new interpreters and found a few promising leads. Though I tried recruiting people who were already certified and working for other agencies, most of them were already committed to one primary agency and only covered other appointments if they had extra time. This was a problem, because I needed interpreters who worked exclusively for me and who could be available on demand—ideally within 15 minutes of getting a call.

To solve the problem, I realized I had to train my own team

instead of trying to poach employees from elsewhere. After considering my options, I decided that a woman named Nuvia, Yesenia's cousin Evelyn and my brother-in-law Matias—all of whom had worked with Yesenia at her office—might be a good fit.

I knew all three of them were great at customer service and spoke excellent English and Spanish. After approaching them about the opportunity, they were all excited to start the process of getting licensed. Though Matias passed both the oral and the written test on his first attempt, Nuvia and Evelyn only passed the written portion. I was glad I could start giving Matias appointments right away, but I had to break the news to Nuvia and Evelyn that they would have to pass the oral exam first.

"I'm sorry," I told Nuvia, "but I know you'll pass the second time and then I'll bring you on. It's just too much risk otherwise."

"I just got nervous during the test," she said, her voice shaking. "Are you sure there's no way? I could really use the work." At that, Nuvia trailed off and started to cry, sending a pang through my heart. She was a single mother recovering from cancer, without a job and unable to provide for her daughter or pay her medical bills. Before I could help myself, I spoke up.

"Maybe I can still use you in the meantime," I said quickly. "But you have to schedule a new oral exam right away, and you can't tell anyone about me doing this—not even Lucio." I knew Nuvia and Lucio were good friends, but I didn't want the word to spread about the risk I was taking. After explaining everything, Nuvia had a huge smile on her face.

"Thank you, Carla!" she replied, giving me a hug. Since I had already bent my own rules and still needed help, I figured that I might as well make the same arrangement with Evelyn. In both cases, since they didn't have provider numbers yet, I filled in Lucio and some of my other certified interpreters' numbers for the time being, so things could keep running smoothly. *They better pass their oral exams on the second try*, I thought.

Aside from the complications with my business, I couldn't believe how well things were going—not just academically but in my relationship as well. Although I'd once told Yesenia that I couldn't see myself in a serious relationship with a woman, I was eating my words; in her, I knew I had found my soulmate. Soon after that realization, I planned a trip for us to Isla Holbox in Mexico, the last virgin island in the Caribbean. When we got there, I proposed to her.

"This is the most romantic activity I've ever done with anyone!" Yesenia said, slipping the ring onto her finger. She didn't know what else to say, so we both chuckled. As always, she was so honest and transparent about her feelings, which made me even crazier about her.

Once the construction on our new condo was completed, Yesenia and I let my mom continue to live in our house in Pasco and rented out the other two rooms, which would help fund our new life. Finally, when our condo was completed and with enough money saved, Yesenia and I moved to Seattle in 2016.

Though Yesenia and I had been together for quite some time, moving to Seattle together was a new beginning because we had never lived alone together. With our life in place and my family tensions at least in a holding pattern, it felt like I was finally ready to fly to new heights.

10

AT THE CROSSROADS

"Opportunity often comes disguised in the form of misfortune or temporary defeat."

—NAPOLEON HILL

Moving to Seattle was just the change I was looking for, and things were going well in school—even if the classes were much harder than they were in community college. I decided to take all the difficult classes first, which would help me keep my options open if I wanted to go to med school and become a psychiatrist instead of a psychologist. It meant that in my first semester, I was taking mathematics, physics and philosophy classes and stretching myself to my limit.

In order to free up enough of my time for school, I put Evelyn in charge of answering calls for The Language Spot, after seeing how organized she was. Still, with me stepping away from the organization, things were not running as smoothly as they were before, and we started dropping more appointments. Even so, I wanted to keep the agency afloat as much as possible since it was my only source of income.

To supplement, I started working part-time as a subcontractor for a big translating agency in Seattle, which let me cover appointments at Seattle Children's Hospital, giving me more exposure to the medical industry in the meantime. At the same time, Yesenia and I were planning our wedding.

Because Yesenia's family was Catholic, we began by getting breakfast with a priest they knew to discuss our options. Though we knew getting married in a church wouldn't be possible because of the Catholic Church's stance on homosexuality, we thought there could be a way for him to attend as a friend.

"We would love to have you there," Yesenia said. "Even if it can't be an official ceremony, maybe you could come as a friend and give us your blessing?"

"I appreciate your kind offer," he said politely, "but unfortunately I have to decline. If I attended your ceremony and anyone in the church found out, I could be defrocked." We were disappointed; Yesenia didn't want him to lose his position in the church, but had thought that as a close family friend, he might've been able to make an exception. Shortly after, I had an idea.

"Babe," I asked, "what if we had a traditional Mayan wedding in the Riviera Maya? It's where our ancestors came from, and they did *not* discriminate against homosexuality." As I explained, male and female homosexuality had only been deemed a sin after the arrival of Spanish conquistadors in Mexico. Mayan culture was so accepting of homosexuality that there was even a patron god named Xochipilli, also known as the Flower Prince, who was thought of as a patron deity of homosexuals.

After explaining everything to Yesenia and talking her through it, she agreed to have a traditional Mayan wedding officiated by shamans—though only under the condition that the shamans not come traditionally dressed in *penachos* and *taparrabos*, ceremonial head crests and loin cloths. Unfortunately, the shamans didn't obey the request—and when the day came, the first thing Yesenia saw on her way to the altar with her extremely Catholic mother was not one, but two nearly naked shamans dancing and burning copal, an incense used for ceremonial purposes.

Our ceremony was in Playa del Carmen, by the beach, with a translator present to translate for the shamans because the whole ceremony was in Mayan. After the ceremonial burning of the copal, the shamans began a traditional prayer and a musician blew into a conch shell, asking for permission, attention and blessings from the four cardinal points

The shamans offered Yesenia and I *balche*, a fermented drink of tree bark and honey, which was intended to nourish our souls. After that, we exchanged yellow and white flowers, which represented the sun and the moon. Then, the shamans tied our hands with red lace to represent the beginning of a true love relationship and our union.

After depositing flowers, cacao, seeds and water in the ground, Yesenia and I washed our feet as a symbol of trust and humility, and the shamans invited our parents and closest family to pray over us. Finally, accompanied by the blowing of a conch shell, drums and the burning of copal, we offered our flowers to the sea—and we shared a kiss to complete the ceremony.

Still feeling high from the beautiful ceremony and a gorgeous honeymoon that followed, I got a call from Nuvia on my way home.

"Carla, I don't know if you know this," she began, "but

there are investigators looking into your business." Hearing this, my stomach dropped. A couple months prior, some of the payment vouchers my company had submitted had been denied. Washington's L&I department had flagged them because they'd noticed that the numbers and names were mismatched and in an old format. They'd requested that we resend the vouchers in their updated format.

Upon hearing this, I asked my receptionist to resubmit three months of vouchers the new way, transferring all the information from the old forms into the new ones, this time changing the names so that they matched the provider numbers. In all, it was worth around $30,000 that I'd already paid the interpreters, so it wasn't a cost I could afford to absorb.

Though I knew that changing the provider numbers was risky and wrong, I had previously done it temporarily with Lucio's permission and it hadn't been an issue. Nobody else seemed to be affected by it, and it seemed like the only person in danger, if anyone, was me. *This is a short-term solution, just like before,* I thought. *It's a way to keep working until I can figure everything out.* But now, it sounded like L&I had found out about what I'd done.

"I'm not sure exactly what they have," Nuvia said, "but they're asking a lot of people a lot of questions." After getting off the phone, I was in a full panic, with my mind spiraling to all kinds of dark places.

"What am I going to do?" I asked Yesenia, with my heart racing and my breath coming short. She grabbed my shoulders to steady me.

"First, take a breath and try to calm down," she said. "I know someone who had a similar issue. Why don't I call him and he can put us in touch with his attorney to give us some advice?" I agreed, and Yesenia made the connection. Later that day, I was on the phone with the attorney, Jim Frush. After explaining my situation, he finally spoke.

"If the investigation proceeds and they find that you've broken the law the way you've described," Jim said, "that's a felony. It won't just mean the end of your company—it could even mean that you'll be deported." If I was anxious before, now I was terrified.

"Still," he continued, "I don't want you to panic. Murphy's Law says, 'If anything can go wrong, it will,' but that doesn't mean you should just sit back and wait to be doomed. It means we need to prepare for the worst, while not letting this take control of your entire life. From experience, these investigations can last *years*—so the best advice I can give you right now is prepare for a long ride, but keep living your life and don't let this consume you." It might've been good advice, but it was easier said than done—at that moment, all I could think about was losing everything I'd ever worked for.

After discussing everything, Jim suggested that I stop submitting any interpreting appointments to L&I and to take extreme action to stop whatever damage had already been done.

"If you close your business down entirely," he said, "I will represent you, and you'll be in a better position as things go forward." At the end of the call, we agreed that I would pay him an upfront retainer fee so that he was available in case anything happened, and that we would re-evaluate everything once he got in touch with the investigators. With that, we ended the phone call, and I sprang into action immediately.

After getting off the phone, I made calls to other interpreters and agencies in my network who could cover whatever remaining business I had and gradually made arrangements to transfer my appointments to them. I started calling my clients and explaining the transition to them, and talking to all the interpreters I'd hired to let them know that I would be closing down. Though the entire process was draining and took a few weeks, I did as my attorney had said. Soon after, The Language Spot was shut down entirely.

I felt lost and defeated. Interpreting was my only source of income and now my business was gone. In a matter of weeks, I went from feeling like I was rising to feeling like I was sinking. As I was mulling over the possibility of being deported, I called my mom to explain my situation and ask for advice.

"You need to change your state of mind if you want the situation to change," she said after hearing all my concerns. "Remember: nothing good will come if you're depressed, anxious and fearful about the future. Everything happens for a reason and we all make mistakes, so take responsibility and ownership. Learn the lesson and trust that everything happens for a reason."

Like my attorney had told me, my mom said that I had already done every practical thing I could do, and I couldn't let the situation ruin my life in the meantime. As she said, I had to try to stay calm and positive, because no matter what outcome was coming my way, I would attract a better one if I remained in a positive state of mind.

At the end of our call, my mom suggested that I also seek some spiritual guidance on top of what I'd already done to prepare. With that in mind, I started looking for someone I thought could give me some clarity about what the future might hold. I remembered that my friend had mentioned a good tarot card reader named Laurie, and had given me her information at a party a while ago.

I searched her online and saw many positive reviews, so I booked an appointment. *If anyone can give me any clues about what's going to happen to me in the future*, I thought, *then I'm more than willing to listen.*

From the first few moments I spent with her, she impressed me by telling me things about myself there was no way she could have known without having some kind of gift. After getting comfortable, I told her everything about what I was going through.

"Can you please tell me what my future holds?" I asked, hopeful for some kind of guidance. After thinking it over for a moment, she spoke.

"A good card reader can't actually tell you your future," she replied, "because there's no such thing as knowing for certain what the future holds. The future has many possibilities, and even a small decision can change the course of things entirely, like a butterfly effect. Tarot is simply a divination tool aided by the presentiment of the future based on the person's current circumstances that gives the reader a set of clues that they must weave into a story."

As I thought her words over, she asked me to try asking a more specific question that the cards might shed light on through their coded astrological wisdom and to shuffle the cards three times. Finally, I had a question.

"Will I get deported as a result of this investigation?" I asked nervously. After my question, I drew a card from the deck as she instructed, which I revealed was The Sun. She explained the many meanings of the card: that the roundness of the sun represented perfection or completion, and that round beings and objects were often thought of as perfect (such as certain cells and planets).

"But The Sun can also mean that things will come to light," Laurie said, "and as long as you are in the right, the situation will turn in your favor." *Fuck*, I thought. *But what if I'm not entirely "in the right?"* I pulled another card: The Chariot.

"There will be some changes ahead," she said. "The Chariot along with the Sun can indicate a speed and decisiveness to things being brought to light. The Chariot brings in new energy and clears out the old, moving beyond the past." I nodded, and she encouraged me to ask another question.

"Will I end up going to medical school?" I asked. Once again, I drew a card from the deck: The Emperor. Again, she explained the card and its meanings: The Emperor was a reigning card, a power card that represented being in charge of a situation and about taking responsibility.

"Let yourself be open to any path that allows you to explore your highest potential," she continued. "You will find the path where you can accomplish that goal, and it will be the path of least resistance—not the one that is the most difficult or complex. If it's a good path for you, it will match your energy and you will feel in flow and harmony with the process. You just have to recognize the path when it shows up in front of you. Your highest potential may be in medical school, but it also might not."

After our meeting ended, I wasn't quite sure what meaning to give what Laurie had just told me. However, even though her words seemed a bit ambiguous, I had strange sense of clarity. Though I'd enjoyed studying psychology and was excited at the possibility to make it into medical school, I was feeling disillusioned and uncertain about my future. I'd already spent a lot of money trying to build a career and put myself in a position to potentially go to medical school—but if I got charged with a felony, I wouldn't be able to practice medicine anyway, and it would all be for nothing.

11

THE CRAFT

"Life isn't about finding yourself. Life is about creating yourself."

—GEORGE BERNARD SHAW

Following the advice of my attorney and my mom, I kept living my life as normally as I could and continued working towards my BA in Psychology. In line with being optimistic about the future and what I could achieve, I had officially decided that I would pursue a pre-med track in spite of whatever doubt was in my mind (and in spite of the workload being akin to a double major).

When I graduated from UW in 2017, I studied as much as I could and took the MCAT test—but when the results came back, I saw I had a 498. The mean score on the MCAT was 500, and it was generally the minimum that most medical schools would accept. Regardless, I still researched and applied to three medical schools in Washington. After a few months of waiting, I had heard back from all three that I hadn't been accepted. If I wanted to go to medical school, I would have to spend several hundred hours studying, retake the eight-hour MCAT and reapply the following year.

Disappointed, I decided I would take a gap year to learn more about myself, save some money and make a clearer decision about the future. While I was thinking things over, Yesenia had transitioned away from her old business and had started working in the mortgage industry as a loan officer.

One day, she got a fully-approved client who wanted to put an offer on a house in Tacoma, Washington, located one hour from Seattle, but wanted to see it one more time. After speaking to the client, Yesenia called a realtor to explain the situation.

"I'm sorry," the realtor explained, "but it's outside of my driving range."

"But the client is putting an offer in," Yesenia said. "You don't have to show multiple homes, and it's pretty much a done deal."

"Sorry, but call me when you have leads in Seattle," the realtor replied. "Tacoma just isn't my area." With that, the realtor hung up, and Yesenia was in shock, making eye contact with me after seeing that I'd overheard some of the call. A little later that evening, she came to me with an idea.

"Babe, what if you got your realtor's license?" she asked. I raised an eyebrow at her. "The woman I just talked to let go of a $15,000 commission because she didn't want to drive 45 minutes." I was in shock.

"I'll drive 45 minutes for $15,000!" I replied. She laughed.

"From what I've gathered so far, I don't think realtors actually *do* very much," she said. "You just have to go and open doors and you can make a lot of money." Though I wasn't entirely sold on it, I did need a way to make some money again. "You already took the MCAT," Yesenia said finally. "The real estate exam should be a lot easier than that by comparison."

At the time, the only frame of reference I had for the real estate industry was through Yesenia, who had just become one of the founding members of the National Association of Hispanic Real Estate Professionals (NAHREP). Still, I had never pictured selling real estate myself.

I was hesitant to jump into real estate rather than trying to work at a lab or a clinic, because the latter would be much better for my med school resume. I had even landed an offer to work at a lab that was doing various psychological tests on monkeys, and it wasn't an easy job to get. Still, I saw that they were planning to pay only $16 an hour, which wasn't even much higher than the minimum wage of $11 an hour.

As I learned online, studying for the real estate exam in Washington would only take about a month. Suddenly, the idea of working as a realtor for a while didn't seem like such a stretch.

I'm likely to only do this during this gap year, I thought to myself. *Just to make a little money before I reapply to med school...but am I going to reapply to med school?* For some reason, my stomach tightened every time I thought of it but every time I thought about calling it quits and doing something else, my mind would stop me.

No, I'd convince myself. *It's too late to quit. All those years of undergrad and months studying for the test for nothing? I can't quit.* This time, Laurie's guidance was floating through my head, and I was thinking a little differently.

I have to let myself be open to the paths where I can explore my highest potential, I thought. *The question is, which path will lead me there?* Eventually, I decided: I would give real estate a try, even if only for a year.

After getting the materials I needed to study for the real estate exam and reviewing them all closely, I scheduled my test and passed it. Because I needed a place to hang my license before going out on my own, I started interviewing with a few brokerages and eventually settled on Keller Williams, which was the one that was closest to where I lived.

On my first days of orientation at Keller Williams, I sat down with my team leader, Mandy. She had short black hair, manicured fingers and a deep, confident voice. She was smiling brightly as she explained her background, which was serving as the personal assistant to Mike Ferry, the founder of The Mike Ferry Organization, which was the global leader of real estate coaching and training.

"So, Carla," she said, "what do you want to accomplish with us this year?"

"I'm not totally sure," I began.

"Well, it's a good time to start thinking about it," she said with a huge smile, pressing her fingers on a sheet labeled "Yearly Goals." Since I'd just graduated college, I'd looked at how much money people could expect to make with my degree and saw jobs that paid around $60,000. Still, I'd heard that real estate agents could make a lot more than that.

"I think I want to make around $100,000," I said. Based on the math I'd done about the local market and the commission that real estate agents made, that sounded like a reasonable number. Still, Mandy looked puzzled.

"Why so little?" she asked, confused. I was trying not to blush. "Why not double that or triple that number? Multiply it by four, even! In real estate, anything is possible." I started laughing.

"Okay, then I want to make $250,000," I said, almost as a joke—based on other research I'd done, that was how much the average psychiatrist made a year in Washington, though achieving that would mean another eight years of school and getting hundreds of thousands of dollars in debt. Mandy gave me a knowing smile and nodded.

"Okay," she continued, "how are you going to accomplish that?" I gulped. Truthfully, I had no idea how I would accomplish it, and I told her as much. "That's okay!" she replied. "We're going to work on your future success together."

After our exchange, she started drawing on the piece of paper in front of us, writing the $250,000 number on top of it. After that, she sketched out the timeline of the year and made notes about how many potential leads I would have to call, plus how many of them I'd have to close and at what prices.

"You can't possibly know where to go if you don't know where you're at now," she began, "so you will have to measure everything. You have to make notes about how many calls you make, how many clients you talk to, how many appointments you get from those calls and how many of those calls you actually close. It's all about numbers!" *She makes it sound so simple*, I thought. *Not easy, but simple.*

"I'm going to teach you the craft, and we're going to start with what I call the 411 cheat," she said. As she explained, it was a system of setting four top goals, then breaking those goals down into what would have to happen every quarter, every month and every week to make them happen. Walking away from our first meeting, I was a little overwhelmed—but Mandy wasn't done giving me advice.

"One of the best things about working with us is there's so much opportunity for education and growth," she said warmly. "In order to get the most out of your time with us and out of real estate in general, you will need to invest in yourself— maybe more than you ever have before. And I think a great way is by taking a course that we have."

As she explained, Keller Williams was hosting a seminar

designed by a renowned speaker named Dianna Kokoszka, which was specifically about learning to invest in yourself for greater success. Dianna had sold 104 homes her first year in real estate by knocking on people's doors, and had sold more than 4,000 houses in her full 27-year career. She was a mogul who was teaching new agents how to do the same things that she did.

Lastly, Mandy explained the seminar would cost $1,600, which I had not expected, and that I would have to miss an entire week of work to attend. Unsure of what to do, I remembered my dad's words echoing in my head: *You can choose the profession you want in life, just make sure you become the best at what you do. Remember: knowledge is power.*

After hearing Mandy talk and seeing how she presented herself, I felt my own energy changing. *Maybe anything really is possible through doing this,* I thought. *The opportunity to learn from someone sharing all the secrets to becoming a millionaire doesn't come every day.*

"I'll go to the conference," I told Mandy finally, figuring I would worry about the money later. She smiled.

"Don't worry about the price of the ticket, by the way," she said with a wink. I just wanted to see if you were committed enough to pay for it yourself. I'll pay for half of your ticket, and we can deduct the other half from your first commission check." With that, she turned and walked away from my cubicle and back to her office.

About a week later, I was attending Dianna Kokoszka's seminar, which was an annual event they called BOLD, which stood for Business Objective: Life by Design. Right away, I felt a little bit out of place—the room was packed with other real estate agents wearing haute couture. The men were in sharp suits with chunky Rolexes and shiny shoes, and the women were in high-end blazers and dresses with Christian Dior bags on their arms and Louboutins on their feet. I had dressed as nicely as I could, of course, but I knew my outfit was probably one of the cheaper ones in the room.

The MC of the event was Cody Gibson—another big figure in the industry—who gave an introduction before playing a recording of Dianna explaining some of her concepts. Even in video form, she was so full of confidence and shared success stories of individual realtors and companies that she'd helped make millions. I took notes as fast as I could.

The strategies they taught throughout were about fine-tuning our closing ratios, as well as strategies on how to scale our numbers to scale our sales.

"It's all about numbers and pushing through to get to a yes more quickly," Cody explained. "In this industry, you have to have a thick skin, but you also have to focus on what's really important, because what you focus on expands. Focus on why you want to close a certain amount of transactions and make a certain amount of money. Focus on your purpose, because ultimately, it isn't about the money. It is about your *why*. What is your *why*? Why are you here?"

As I pondered his words, I realized that I had answered that question many times throughout the process of applying to medical school—but even though I was almost 30, I still didn't feel like I had the answer. What *was* my purpose? Why was I here? Meanwhile, Cody continued to drill down on the relationship between wealth and purpose.

"Whose problems would I solve if I gave you a check for $50,000?" Cody asked. Everyone raised their hands at once. He nodded.

"I can assure you that we all have very different salaries in this room," he said. "Some of you earn $200,000, $500,000 or a million dollars a year. And yet most of us still feel like we need more to be happier. The reality is: you don't. You actually need to be clearer about what your goals are and what you want in life."

"In this course," he continued, "I *am* going to teach you how to become a millionaire—but I'm also going to teach you how to lead a balanced life and a life that you design on your own terms." Later on, he made us visualize our future and write a letter to ourselves that we would give to the staff, a letter that they would mail back to us exactly one year from that date.

As the teachers explained, we were to write a letter congratulating ourselves on all our accomplishments for the following year as if they had already happened, and to picture why they made us happy.

"Affirmations in the present tense are more believable," Cody said, "and they inspire you to take action towards your dreams. Your subconscious mind does not understand time, and it does not distinguish between present and future, so it is always better to use the present tense." With all the instructions in mind, I began to write:

Dear future me,

I am very proud about everything you have accomplished this year. I can't believe it's not even the end of the year and you just cashed a commission check that made you cross your $250K goal! It makes me so happy to see you travel, spend quality time with your wife and help your mom economically so she doesn't have to work as much. Congratulations on purchasing your brand new AMG G-Wagon with red interiors!

Carla Moreno

After I was done, I sealed the letter and handed it to the staff. Finally, Cody broke the silence in the room again.

"Everything starts with a thought," he said. "Here's how Napoleon Hill puts it: 'The starting point of all achievement is desire. Keep this constantly in mind. Weak desires bring weak results, just as a small fire makes a small amount of heat.' In our case, you need to know your deep desire that will fuel your career."

Towards the end of the week-long seminar, he mentioned a list of 15 books he encouraged everyone in the room to read.

"If you get nothing else from this seminar," he said, "you should read the books on this list—*particularly Think and Grow Rich* by Napoleon Hill. No book has made more millionaires than that one has." When the seminar was over, I ordered all the books he had mentioned, determined to consume them all.

Following his advice, I started to read *Think and Grow Rich* and was immediately enthralled. The book was captivating. In each chapter, Napoleon Hill referred to a "secret" at least once—but he never specifically named what the actual secret was. As he explained, it was more beneficial and penetrating not to reveal the secret, but to allow readers to get to it themselves. For some, he wrote, it would happen almost immediately. For others, it might take multiple readings.

Despite the book's title, I realized that it was not only about increasing income and becoming rich. It was actually a very spiritual book about putting mind before matter, the same concept that Dr. Leenards had taught all his clients. It was also the same thing my mom had been telling me ever since I was a kid: *If you can see it in your mind, you can hold it in your hand.* Even though the book was written in 1937, the lessons were still as relevant as ever.

As I worked my way through the books on Cody's list, I felt

my mindset gradually changing. Although I had run businesses before, I had never done it with a clear path in mind. I had never set clear, concrete goals; I was always hustling without any clear direction. Now, I was realizing that I was in control of setting that direction myself.

Similarly, as I got to know more of the women I was working with, I was shocked by how collaborative they were compared to the culture of interpreting. When I was trying to get my agency off the ground, none of my competitors were sharing information. If anything, they were hiding their business secrets as closely as they could. Many of the realtors I was getting acquainted with at Keller Williams were making *way* more money than many of the interpreters and agency owners I knew, and yet they were willing to tell anyone *anything* about how to do it themselves.

Since I was just getting started, my team lead had given me a list of actions I could take to grow my business, which was laid out as a pie chart. According to her, if I did two or three things from their chart, I was almost sure to get two or three closings a month—and one of the first things was calling 100 different people *a day*. Other tips were to do open houses every weekend, contact everyone in your social sphere to let them know you were in the business and calling canceled and expired listings.

Although I explored all of their suggestions, the one I focused on most was doing tons of cold calls, which felt like a brute-force method of getting good at sales. In order to do the calls, the brokerage gave all its realtors a sales script that was formatted like a flow chart.

Instead of calling 100 people a day, I sometimes called 500 people by using a calling software that allowed multiple calls at once to see who would answer first. In general, I was calling people who lived close to recently sold homes to tell them how good the market was for sellers, sometimes with Mandy listening in to give me advice. My goal was to talk to at least 20 people a day. While not everyone answered, when they did, I would set into my sales script:

"Hi! This is Carla Moreno with Keller Williams International Realty," I would say, "and I wanted you to be one of the first to hear that your neighbor just sold his home for $150,000 over the asking price. Have you considered *selling your home?*" Given the way I would present it on the phone, I got a few common replies:

"No, thank you."

"If I were to even consider selling my home, I can assure you it would not be through someone who cold-called me."

"Fuck off!"

After overhearing one of my calls, Mandy gave me some advice.

"Make it down-pitched when you say 'selling your home,'" she said, "otherwise you'll sound insecure when you say it." Every morning as Mandy would hear my colleagues and I making our sales calls, she would cheerfully encourage us from her office. "Every no gets you closer to a yes!" she shouted. "Remember: the secret is in the numbers!"

At first, the calls were so rough that I got too embarrassed to do them at the office in front of the other realtors, and started doing them from home. Though Yesenia was usually out of the house at 9 am every day, sometimes she stayed home and over-heard my calls—and as she told me, some of them were painful to listen to because whenever a client objected to me, I would freeze.

"Why would I choose you?" one of the callers said to me. "You're cold-calling me because you probably have no business!"

Though the rejections stung, I started collecting the most

common ones I heard when calling expired listings, writing them down and adding them to a sales script. I also wrote out my own responses to them and compiled them into a Rolodex for future calls.

Eventually, if someone said, "You're the 20th agent who has called me about this," I would flip through my Rolodex for the perfect response to handle their objection. Finally, I would reply, "Well, now you know there are at least 20 agents who work hard to find business and *I* am one of them. *I* work just as hard to sell the homes I list, so how about we meet for coffee or lunch to discuss what I will do differently to get your home sold this time?" After running my scripts hundreds of times, I got my first yes.

"Sure," a lady on the phone said. "Let's meet at the property today at 3 pm." There was a gong at the office we were supposed to ring every time someone set an appointment with a potential client—and finally, I got to ring it. The whole office cheered.

In my first month, I closed two transactions, just as Mandy promised I would if I followed the instructions. At the end of the month, she came by with two commission checks.

"Congratulations!" she said warmly. "I told you they would be nice and fat. You deserve it!" As I soon saw, not all agents closed two transactions a month, made it through 100 calls a day or spent their weekends at open houses. Not everyone had the stamina to persist through so many rude comments on cold calls. Still, just as Mandy had said, it was a numbers game. The faster I got through painful calls, the faster I got at handling objections and closing deals. Learning the craft wasn't easy, but it was simple: it only took consistency and dedication.

A few months later, Keller Williams planned another convention with Gary Keller himself, one of the founders of the company—and this time, Dianna Kokoszka would also be attending in person.

"If you liked the BOLD conference," Mandy told me, "this one is going to blow your mind." Since the first one was so exciting, I talked Yesenia and my sister-in-law Sandra into coming to it as well. Yesenia had also told Sandra the story about the realtor who wouldn't drive to Tacoma, and it had been enough to encourage Sandra to join the industry as well.

My business seed had truly taken root, and I was investing in myself as much as I could. I decided I would read even more and take even more courses until I knew everything about the industry, front and back. *I'm going to learn so much that customers never even think to ask about my experience,* I thought. I would get as many different real estate certifications as possible.

As it turned out, there were many different ways to specialize as a realtor. I could focus on first-time home buyers, veterans, the elderly, real estate investors or break into the luxury market.

While I was learning more life-changing things faster than I ever had before, I was still finding it difficult to get listings, which meant working with sellers. Instead, I was mostly stuck working with buyers.

"Listings give you more leverage," Mandy would always say. "You can easily have five listings each month, whereas you couldn't possibly work with five buyers at the same time. Buyers take more time and it's easier to scale with sellers, so focus on getting more listings first."

When it came to doing interviews with people looking to sell their homes and trying to get those listings, there was almost invariably one dreaded question:

"So, how long have you been a realtor?"

After telling them that I'd only been practicing for a few months, the sellers would lose interest.

"I know I've only been in the industry for three months," I'd explain, "but I've already sold six homes."

"I'm sorry, honey," the sellers would say, "but we prefer going with someone who has a bit more experience."

From all the work I was putting in, I was starting to land appointments but I wasn't actually closing deals. In other words, I couldn't make anyone actually pick me as their agent to sell their home. I had already gone to 13 listing appointments and I still didn't have any listings.

"Babe," I asked Yesenia one day, "Mandy says listings are a numbers game and I should have already landed one by now. Can I practice with you so you can tell me if I'm doing anything wrong?"

"Sure," she replied. "Let's do it." With that, I walked outside and pretended to be knocking on the door for a listing appointment. Finally, Yesenia opened the door and I smiled broadly.

"Hello!" I said enthusiastically. "Thanks for having me over and giving me the opportunity to list your home." I was proud of myself for memorizing the script, including the down pitch on "list your home"—I had recently read more about the power of tonality and was eager to apply it.

"Um, of course," Yesenia replied, unsure of what to say.

"Let me tell you what makes us stand out at Keller Williams," I said, pulling out my laptop for a full presentation. After that, I started explaining everything that would make a house sell or not and what kind of marketing we could do—but before I was even three minutes in, my wife's eyes were wandering.

"What's wrong?" I asked, a little frustrated.

"Nothing!" she said. "Please, continue!"

"Is it bad?"

Yesenia took a breath—I could tell she was trying as hard as she could to let me finish, but whatever I was doing wasn't working.

"Babe, I didn't mean to interrupt you but...it's *really* bad," she replied. My face fell. I had been practicing for my listing appointment for weeks to memorize everything, and I even had flashcards for every possible scenario as I entered the home. How could what I was doing be bad? I was following Dianna's proven script!

Though I was a little disappointed, I tried my best to swallow my ego and hear her feedback. As she explained, the issue was that I was giving too much information too quickly— and that I was hitting her with too many sales techniques too fast, which made me sound like a robot.

"In school, we learned this exercise called 'sell me this pen,'" Yesenia said. "The biggest mistake salespeople made was to say, 'This is the best pen in the world, it writes upside down,' and so on, because none of that matters if the person doesn't need a pen in the first place. The best advice I learned in business school was to talk less and listen more—it's why we have two ears and one mouth."

I couldn't deny that what she was saying made sense. I knew Yesenia was a great saleswoman, as she'd been going door to door with her mom selling tamales to strangers ever since she was nine years old. Her own efforts in the lending industry had been growing steadily and she'd just won an award for being "Rookie of the Year." *It's no wonder I'm not getting any listings,* I thought finally.

I took a breath and re-centered myself, trying to get out of my ego and take the advice to heart. Even so, I was determined not to be discouraged. Being open to feedback was not my greatest strength, but I knew I needed to get out of my head if I wanted to improve.

After our practice that morning, I had an appointment with my actual customer. Although I was deviating from the script and I had completely changed my strategy from what I'd practiced for months, I still felt more secure in myself. I followed Yesenia's advice to talk less and listen more.

If the client asked a question, I gave information—but not all at once. I was confident that I knew my objectives, my data and my numbers, but I still waited for them to ask before launching into everything. Finally, at the end, the woman I'd spoken to agreed to give me her listing—my first one ever, five months into my first year.

By the time June came, I had already made my initial goal of $60,000, with only half the year over, which I couldn't believe. Originally, my goal of earning $250,000 had seemed unreachable. Now, seeing how much progress I had made so quickly, I was starting to believe I could accomplish it.

12

THE VINE OF THE DEAD

> *"The Universe is Mental—held in the Mind of THE ALL."*
>
> — *THE KYBALION*

Given the new excitement and possibility that had come into my life, the idea of dropping it all to go back to medical school was beginning to feel less and less appealing. I liked real estate a lot, but I still wanted to find a way to learn more about higher consciousness and behavior. I wanted to find a way to apply my knowledge to help people; maybe it would even help me repair the relationship with my dad.

I had started taking a few prep tests and practice courses again so I could retake the MCAT, but I was quickly losing my enthusiasm. If there was a chance everything could just be taken away from me through the L&I investigation, then what was the point of working so hard—especially when I had potentially found another path for myself in real estate? Then I got an unexpected call from my family.

"Carla, I have sad news," my dad told me. "Your sister Sandy just passed away." As he explained, she'd died from gastrointestinal bleeding a few weeks after having gastric bypass surgery. Hearing it put me in shock. We weren't the closest, but we were still sisters—and she was still so young. After our phone call, I took the first flight to Guadalajara that I could so I could get there in time for her funeral.

After the service, I waited in line with the other attendees to see Sandy lying in her coffin, feeling so many things. I wanted to go back in time and take back all the hurtful things I'd said to her after I found out about the fake Facebook profile she made. She must've been in pain over it, and I never told her I was sorry. Now, it was too late.

When it was over and I returned to Seattle, it felt like my world had been shaken. Nobody had expected Sandy to die so soon; all I could think was how uncertain life could be, and how important it was to spend your time in an intentional, purposeful way. It called more attention to the fact that I'd been putting off the decision about what to do with my future for too long.

At a party shortly after, I spoke to my friend Tanya about the hard decisions I was facing. Like me, she liked learning about expanding consciousness through ancient rituals and sacred medicines.

"I think I know what will help you get some clarity," she told me excitedly.

"Well, I already tried tarot reading and didn't get much from that," I joked.

"Girl, no!" she said. "This is different, you have no idea. Have you ever heard of ayahuasca?" I had taken a class about drugs and behavior in college and learned that ayahuasca was a plant-based psychedelic, commonly used for spiritual and religious purposes by Amazonian tribes.

In ceremonies, a shaman or experienced healer would brew together leaves from different plants which released DMT, a powerful, naturally occurring hallucinogenic compound. According to the books I'd read, the ceremony was for people who wanted to know more about the universe, and it had been around for as long as anyone could remember.

"I've heard of it," I replied.

"Dude, you should do it!" Tanya said. "I just came back from a ceremony with a shaman from Brazil and my experience was mind-blowing. Whatever I thought I knew before that ceremony was like a speck of dust, and ayahuasca helped me see the real vastness of the multidimensional universe we live in." It seemed like she was still in shock from her experience.

"You sound a bit crazy right now," I said jokingly. "Don't they call it the vine of the dead because it brings up your darkest fears and the hallucinations make them seem real?"

"Yes," she replied, "but also because it can connect you to your ancestors and let you speak with them. Plus, if you face your darkest fears, you only do it so you can heal and connect to your multidimensional self, raise your vibration and claim your inner power." She clenched her fist, like she was giving a motivational speech.

"And how is this supposed to help me decide if I should go to medical school or not?" I asked, confused.

"That I don't know, but I have a feeling you might find some answers," she replied confidently. "Just set your intention and ask the goddess Pachamama for the clarity you need. She'll show you what you need to know." I wasn't sure what that meant, but I was intrigued.

"I have to go to Brazil for this?" I asked.

"No, the shaman comes from Brazil," she said. "And luckily

for you, she's coming back next month!" Yesenia was standing nearby, and upon hearing this, she turned and interrupted us.

"Please, babe," she said, not quite jokingly, "no more shamans."

"Tanya was telling me about her ayahuasca experience," I told Yesenia. "Can we try it?" In truth, I had briefly considered doing ayahuasca before Yesenia and I got married while we were down in the Mayan Riviera, but our wedding planner had advised against it. As she explained, some people got *too* much clarity from the ceremony and canceled their weddings altogether. Tanya saw that this was an opportunity to convince her.

"Yesenia," she said seriously, "I have a feeling that if you two do an ayahuasca ceremony together, you will both find so much clarity. Your careers will *blow up!*" Her words sounded a bit ominous, but as she explained, her retreat had given her enormous clarity about pursuing a career focused on developing mental and physical strength.

Shortly after, she started training as a bodybuilder and competed in a national tournament three months later, against people who had been training for upwards of 10 years. She had developed so much muscle that she won first place in three different categories, despite her relative inexperience. By the end of our conversation, Yesenia had politely declined to take part in the ceremony, but she supported me in doing it myself.

Shortly after the party, I opened an email from Tanya that included information from the Brazilian shaman:

Hello my brothers and sisters!

You are invited to participate in our Umbandaime prayer, come to connect with the sacred energies to celebrate, heal and practice self-knowledge. The word "umbanda" comes from a language originated in Ango-

la/Africa, and it means "magic," or "another dimension of life where the spirits live." It also translates to "the unlimited limit, Divine Principle, radiant light, the fountain of eternal life, constant evolution."

The simplest way to define Umbanda is it is "a religion of the people."

The email went on to explain a brief history of the religion, noting that psychic phenomena were universal and had always existed throughout space and time. It also explained the principle of spiritualism, the qualifications of the shaman, what the ceremony would entail and what it could do for those who respected its sacredness.

This is exactly *what I need*, I thought, as soon as I finished digesting the information.

After showing Yesenia documentaries about ayahuasca and showing her different articles about it, I still couldn't convince her to do it. Still, when the day of the retreat came, she relented and decided to come with me.

"I'm nervous about this whole thing," she said, "but I want to be there to support you. Plus, what if you end up finding the clarity Tanya was talking about and then you get super ripped afterward? I don't want to be left behind!" she joked. I laughed, excited that she was coming with me and that we'd be doing it together.

When the day of the retreat finally arrived, we drove into the woods to a cabin in Snoqualmie, a small town in northwest Washington. We arrived with white ceremonial clothing and flower offerings, just as the shaman had instructed us. At 6 pm that evening, the ceremony began.

After the space was prepared and blessed by the shaman by chanting and burning ceremonial candles, the first of several ancestral medicines, ayahuasca, was offered to all the participants. There were about 13 of us altogether and each of us was handed an initial dose in a plastic shot glass. The liquid tasted unpleasant in my mouth, both earthy and bitter as it went down.

"Thank you, mama ayahuasca," I said, as instructed. "Please give me the clarity I need in my life right now."

Once everyone had finished their dose, we were all instructed to get up and dance to the sound of live drums so the energy could flow into our bodies and we would start to feel the medicine's effects.

"Life is music, and music is life," said the shaman. After dancing for about 20 minutes, the mood in the room changed. Some people started to vomit, others ran to the bathroom with diarrhea. Still, the shaman was unfazed, assuring everyone that this was normal.

"This is the purge," she said. "It is a means of purifying and healing a polluted mind and body of afflictive psychic entities." Many of the people in the room were descending into fear, anxiety and paranoia. On the other hand, Tanya, who had also decided to attend (making it her third ayahuasca ceremony), seemed euphoric.

"I don't understand," a frightened girl across the room said between vomiting. "I've done this many times and have never had a bad trip like this."

"Every experience is different because the medicine gives you what you need, sister, not what you want," the shaman explained calmly. "Breathe deeply and open yourself up to see what you need to heal."

Seeing all of this happen around me, I was afraid—not for myself, but for my wife. What had I done by talking her into this? What was going to happen to her? I wasn't feeling anything myself yet, but I wanted to stay alert in case things went badly for her.

After about an hour of chanting and dancing, the time came for the second dose, and I turned to Yesenia.

"Babe, how are you feeling?" I asked. "Are you sure you're okay for a second dose?"

"I'm fine, baby!" she replied, blissful and happy. It seemed that she also wasn't fully experiencing anything yet. With that, we both took a second shot, and within 20 minutes, we were both starting to feel a change. We all laid down in our sleeping bags in a circle around the altar, with the shaman chanting again.

I felt myself melting into the floor, my body becoming fluid and vibrating in unison with the drums. Even so, I was resisting the medicine's full power; I didn't want to lose myself in case Yesenia needed me. I reached to grab her hand when the shaman came up to me and whispered in my ear.

"She's going to be fine," she said, gently separating our hands. "Everyone has to go on their own individual journey, and you won't be able to if you're holding hands."

Almost immediately after separating us, I let myself go and my trip began.

I was running through a neon-colored forest, with plants and animals that looked nothing like I had ever seen. After some time, the spirits of people who had passed away appeared before me— including my sister, Sandy. Seeing her in front of me filled me with emotion. Everything surrounding her passing had happened so fast that we had never had a chance to apologize for the ways we'd hurt each other, and to work out our differences. Now, I was able to embrace her the way I never had, and I felt our spirits forgive each other. Soon, it was time for more medicines.

The next thing we had to take was kambo, the venomous

secretions of an Amazonian tree frog that was said to be a powerful natural antibiotic, capable of boosting the immune system. To administer it, the shaman burned three small circles on our skin and applied the frog's secretions in a paste, since the flesh had to be open to take in the medicine.

As soon as it was applied, I felt an instant rush through my body—a wave of heat that ascended all the way to my head. My blood vessels were dilating, and it felt like my blood pressure was plummeting, making me nauseous and forcing me to vomit.

"Be strong and push through," the shaman said. "This will only last a few minutes. After you purge, you will experience feelings of cleanliness, lightness, quiet and inner peace." With that, we went into our final phase of the trip, beginning around 2 am and lasting about four hours.

In the middle of it all, I felt the presence of many voices through an entity I recognized. It was Ganesha, the Hindu god with the head of an elephant (which was strange, since I'd grown up Catholic). Though he appeared before me, he didn't speak to me. I imagined speaking to him and asking him questions about my life, but instead of giving me an answer, he would respond by taking me back to the past. After re-visiting some of those moments, I was finding answers slowly coming to me.

Finally, I tried to ask about my future—and I got a vision of someone who seemed to be my future self.

I was outside on the balcony of a beautiful, colonial hotel, drinking my morning coffee and getting ready to give a speech. I turned to look inside the hotel room and there was Yesenia, sitting on the sofa and reading a book in our suite, supporting me as always.

Through all of it, I had a sense of achieving transcendence. In my vision, I knew that I was going to do something to encourage others in a field I was passionate about. I knew I would spread my knowledge and share my experience about *something very empowering to me*—but it didn't feel like it involved medical school.

Somehow, I saw that the part of me that wanted to go to medical school was connected to my ego—the part that wanted to have a reputable profession that you had to be "smart" to attain. I wasn't going to medical school because I had a deep love and passion for medicine. I knew I wanted to do *something* with the mind, consciousness and behavior, but it wasn't necessarily becoming a medical doctor.

I also saw my relationship with my dad through a different lens. In a sense, I understood that he had his own shadows and mental programming that perhaps triggered some of his behavior subconsciously. Maybe he was doing the best he could with the the tools he had. I decided that though I would still have clear boundaries with him, I would try to understand him more.

Shortly after the retreat, Yesenia and I took a trip to Acapulco with my mom, who had been reconnecting with her siblings and my godparents—who had a very successful business in Mexico City. We went to my cousin's wedding in Tepoztlan, a beautiful magic town close to the city, and when the wedding was over, my *padrinos* invited us to their condo in Acapulco.

While there, Yesenia and I sat in their jacuzzi and took in a beautiful sunset on the beach. On the horizon, we could see the silhouette of my godparents and my mom playing cards, laughing and enjoying life. My mom seemed so happy. I hadn't seen her laugh that way in years.

In our entire family, my godparents were the only ones who had become millionaires by owning a successful business, and my mom was very proud of them. With the wealth they had created, they helped my grandmother retire, shortly before she passed away at age 63. Looking at them in that moment, I had a realization: I wanted to be like them. I wanted to travel and enjoy life the way they did.

"Babe," I said to Yesenia, "let's become millionaires like my *padrinos*." I knew Yesenia shared the same vision, and so we started a long conversation about our finances, our mutual goals and the life we wanted to live. At the end of our discussion, I decided that medical school was not the right avenue to pursue the life I really wanted. That night, we decided that we wanted to work hard and become wealthy enough to retire by the time I was 35 and Yesenia was 38. After that, we would travel the world and live off of our passive income.

"Also," Yesenia added, "I would like to have a beach house. I want to wake up and drink my morning coffee with this view." I nodded along with her. We didn't know the *how* of our shared dream yet. Still, we knew what we wanted, and we had declared it to the universe.

13

THE CIRCLE OF FIVE

"You're the average of the five people you spend the most time with."

—*JIM ROHN*

After processing my decision, I broke the news to my family and friends that I wasn't going to medical school. Although my mom was very proud of my studies and was already telling all her clients about her "daughter who was going to be a doctor," she still supported my decision to pursue a new career path.

"I'm sure you'll be able to apply many of the things you learned about psychology with your clients," she said. "Understanding people's behaviors and needs will give you an advantage in your sales career, Carlita." I knew she was saying it to make me feel better for choosing a path that didn't require a college degree. All the same, I appreciated her support.

Shortly thereafter, Yesenia told me about a woman she had met named Adriana.

"I think you'd like her," she said. "She's another one of the founding members of NAHREP and she's coming to an event this week—you should make sure you come so you can meet her!"

I took her advice, and when I got to the event, I immediately saw Adriana holding court and having lively conversations with the other real estate professionals who were in attendance. After seeing me across the room, Yesenia ushered me over and introduced us.

"I've heard great things about you!" Adriana said, with a huge smile.

After getting acquainted, I could see why Yesenia thought we would get along. As we talked about our experiences, I realized we thought similarly about certain things; we both had big dreams and goals, and our souls connected right away. We had a similar sense of humor as well.

"You should come work at Sotheby's with me," she said excitedly. "It's a great brand and there's a ton of opportunity right now." As we talked, I explained what I had been through so far in my first five months in the business, as well as all the things I'd learned, certifications I'd gotten and the deals I closed. She was impressed.

"You know what?" she said finally. "I thought I wanted to recruit you, but I don't think you need to be part of a team. You're ready to fly solo." I was surprised to hear her say that, since I hadn't been in the business for very long. "You should still come to meetings with my team, but you don't need to split your commissions with me. I'll answer your questions, but you should do it on your own."

I left the event feeling more excited for the future than I ever had before. At Keller Williams, I was working on a team of realtors and was contributing 50 percent of each of my paychecks as a result. In a way, it felt like the tuition I was paying to attend a real estate university of sorts. At Sotheby's, as Adriana had explained, the breakdown would be better, but it was still a decision I wanted to think through carefully.

Since I'd been with Keller Williams for a while, I had gotten a feel for how the company worked. They were a good place for new agents, because they gave a lot of training and encouragement. Still, there were some drawbacks as well.

At each office there was a designated broker, who was essentially a manager there to help agents with questions about contracts and to give sales advice. Unfortunately, since Keller Williams was such a big outfit, it was hard to get in touch with the designated manager if anything went wrong.

Similarly, one of the big sales hooks for being on a team was that doing so meant you would get leads to pursue without doing as much work on your own—but as I had learned, these leads were usually pretty bad.

Often, it was people who were going on Zillow to look at houses but who weren't all that serious about buying, people who were on unemployment, family homes that had been sitting on the market for a long time and so on. Most of the people I was repping were coming from my own sphere, or from my own work making cold calls.

I knew moving to Sotheby's would mean more access to luxury real estate, which I was excited about, as well as a better cut. I did some math. The typical commission on a house was between two or three percent, and at Sotheby's, my split would be better, particularly because I wasn't going to be in a team anymore that I had to split 50 percent of my commission with.

Given Adriana's encouragement and the numbers, I decided it was time to make the leap to Sotheby's.

With the luxury brand of Sotheby's behind me, I was full of

a new confidence. Just as I had at Keller Williams, I got a list of expired listings and began making my calls—only this time, each of the properties was worth upwards of a million dollars. Though seeing the bigger price tags was a little intimidating, the process was still the same and advice I'd gotten from Mandy and others still applied: it was a numbers game.

After browsing listings and calling many numbers—including Seattle-based rapper Macklemore—I built enough confidence to land an appointment for a $1.89 million expired listing in Escala, an upscale condominium tower in downtown Seattle. Though getting the appointment was great, it didn't fix the problem that I had no experience in the luxury market, and thus very little chance of actually winning the listing. I knew I needed to reach out to someone for help.

After looking through the paperwork I'd gotten with my leads, I called the number for my designated broker to get some assistance. When he picked up, I introduced myself and set into a pitch.

"I'm still getting experience with luxury listings," I said, "so I'd love to partner with an agent on this, if they were willing to teach me some things and come to the listing appointment with me. I'd also split my commission with whoever agrees to it. Could you connect me to someone?"

Sure enough, a few minutes later, I got a call from a realtor named Chris who was interested in my offer and agreed to meet me at the listing appointment. When the day came, Chris and I showed up early to meet in person and get acquainted.

When we met with the client, Chris and I had already developed some natural chemistry and were working well together—and when it was over, the client had given us the listing! Next, I'd have to hustle to get the condo sold, but with Chris promising to advise me, I felt confident that I could do it.

Since I'd made the decision to focus on real estate, I had a new level of clarity and was pushing harder than ever towards my goals. I'd been making quick progress since I started in January 2018, but I had a long way to go to achieve my financial goal for the year.

I soon heard that NAHREP was putting together another event and had booked a speaker named Thatch Nguyen, a relatively well-known figure in Seattle real estate. The event was going to be a networking and mingling situation with a keynote presentation about real estate investing.

Just like the presentation that Dianna Kokolzska gave for Keller Williams, Thatch had an incredible stage presence and so much valuable information to give. Thatch explained the BRRRR method, which stood for Buy, Rehab, Rent, Refinance and Repeat. As he explained, real estate investors could find a property that needed significant repairs, buy it and add value to it by rehabbing it. After that, they could rent it and refinance the mortgage afterwards to get the equity out of it, and then start the process over again on another house using the same money.

In addition to the information he gave, he also shared his personal story of how he and his father had fled Vietnam 40 years before with only $100 between them. Now, he was a multi-millionaire, earning more than a million dollars a year in passive income.

I was furiously taking notes the entire time and collecting countless epiphanies—even if it didn't seem like everyone else in the room was having the same experience. Afterwards, I mingled with the other attendees.

"He was good, right?" a realtor asked me casually.

"What he was teaching was incredible!" I replied. "I thought that was pure gold." The realtor raised her eyebrows, a little surprised at my enthusiasm. After our brief conversation, I moved through the crowd, looking for Thatch. When I finally made it to him, I shook his hand with a huge smile.

"That was so amazing," I said. "You're so inspirational. Do you have any more teachings on this?" He smiled and explained that he actually had an entire course on it, before giving me a business card.

"I actually have an event for these same topics next week," he replied. "You should come."

And so, the next week, I went to Thatch's orientation event for his course, which was a much smaller group of people than the conference had been. After his initial talk, we broke into smaller groups and got to spend some one-on-one time with him discussing our unique situations. Finally, it was my turn.

"Everything we've discussed about growing wealth in real estate is important," Thatch said, "but it won't work without a clear *why*. What is your *why*, Carla?"

As I pondered this once again, I thought back to the discussion Yesenia and I had had in Acapulco. Though we were both eager to make money and create a bright future together, we'd paid for our wedding ourselves using credit cards, and we were still paying off the debt. Living in the city was expensive, and we often only had enough money to cover our expenses with little left over to save. I needed help to achieve my dream of traveling with Yesenia—and taking care of my mom.

She had already been through hell leaving my dad and things had gotten even worse for her recently. My mom had just had two serious accidents, one where she almost lost an eye and another where she fractured her back. After all the support she'd given me, it hurt to think of her rebuilding her life once again, just to find a way to retire.

"I want to achieve financial freedom so my wife and I can travel more, and so I can assist my mom in her retirement," I said finally. "I want her to be able to stop working and to support her." Thatch looked at me and smiled, seeming to connect with what I'd said.

"That is a great, big *why*," he said. "Unfortunately, my dad passed away before I could retire him, but my big *why* for becoming a millionaire was to help my mom retire. For that reason, I'm going to help you."

From that moment on, Thatch began to mentor me in real estate and teach me ways to grow my wealth and develop my mindset. In another one of his meetups, I met another investor my age named Jan, who was particularly good at analyzing the numbers on deals and breaking down whether something would end up profitable or not.

As he explained, he'd been buying properties and turning them into Airbnbs. He was now making good passive income by applying the BRRRR method. At the end of our meeting, he handed me a business card.

"Take this," he said. "If you ever have any questions on a deal you're putting together, call me. I'll analyze anything you want for $100 an hour."

The conversations Yesenia and I had about real estate and our finances had already been pushing us in a positive direction, but Thatch and Jan's influence was helping even more. Instead of only thinking about representing buyers and sellers as a real estate agent, I was thinking more about how to break into investing—and we were working harder than ever to accomplish our goals of traveling more and purchasing a waterfront property.

I was working 12 hours a day, and Yesenia was typically working the same or more. We tried to find precious time to spend together whenever we could, but the reality was that we were both trying as hard as we could to make money and get out of debt.

After reading more books about investing and thinking

about what we'd learned from Thatch, we were eager to take out a loan against our condo equity and put it towards our first major investment project. Soon after, Yesenia saw a listing on Facebook Marketplace and called me over. It was a plot of undeveloped land with enough space to develop six lots, and it cost $120,000 for the parcel.

"I have a great idea," she said excitedly. "What if we bought this lot, subdivided it and put a manufactured house on each of the lots?"

"That sounds cool," I said hesitantly, "but we have zero experience subdividing lots or developing them. It sounds a bit complicated for a first project, don't you think?"

"I think we can do it," she replied. "When I was growing up, my mom would buy lots and manufactured homes on auction, place manufactured homes on each one with a permanent foundation underneath and sell each one for a great profit. We can easily do the same thing."

When Yesenia's parents came to the US, they were determined to make sure their family was financially stable, which meant learning how to grind. Her parents had to learn how to invest and how to make a little money go a long way.

After hearing her explanation, Yesenia convinced me: we could take a Home Equity Line of Credit (HELOC) against our condo for $120,000, the maximum we could borrow, which would cover the cost of the land. After that, she had another $40,000 line of credit through her business that she could use to purchase a manufactured home, develop one of the lots and sell it with the house attached. From the profit on that lot, we would develop a second one, and so forth, until we could finance the entire project. Finally, we also had $20,000 in personal credit lines between us for any additional expenses we might face.

With a plan in place, we moved forward with purchasing

the lot and looking into subdividing it—but we soon realized that the process was much more complicated (and expensive) than we'd anticipated. Yesenia's mom's lots had been in rural areas, but we were developing in the city, and it was *much* more expensive. In a rural area, all you needed to develop was a septic tank and a connection to electricity. In our case, we would have to pave the road, make street improvements—like sidewalks and street lights—and pay school taxes.

The worst part was that we couldn't develop just *one* lot. We had to pay for the entire subdivision all at once, which was not cheap. Between purchasing the land and analyzing what we could do with it, we got a revised quote of $260,000 to finish the project—which we knew we wouldn't be able to do ourselves.

Shortly after, Yesenia called her mom and her two older sisters to ask if they might be interested in coming in with us. Since I had already taken multiple real estate courses, I had a better grasp of how to create spreadsheets and analyze deals, so I gave everyone a presentation of what they could hope to earn and what their ownership percentages would be. Our potential profit was estimated to be 40 percent in two years, or 20 percent annualized. As I'd recently learned, the average return from investing in the stock market was only 10 percent a year, so anything higher was amazing for a first deal.

After hearing our entire presentation, they all said yes—and after raising money from Yesenia's two sisters and their husbands, her parents and my mom (who had recently won a medical settlement), we had all the extra money we needed to finish the project.

With the money in place, I set to work about learning the process of subdividing land into lots. After that, Yesenia's sister Sandra was going to take over, develop each lot and put manufactured homes on them, since she had prior experience with this process. However, we found out that the manufactured homes we were going to buy were more expensive than we thought, and buying them outright would've left only a tiny margin after a ton of work. Fortunately, Yesenia's mom had a great idea.

"These homes are expensive because we're looking at them only as retail buyers," she said. "What if we got a dealership license so we could buy the homes directly from the factory instead of through a third party?" After hearing those words, Yesenia and I perked up—if we managed to do that, we'd be getting the homes at a 30 to 40 percent discount! Of course, getting a dealership license for the homes would be its own headache, but we all agreed it was the best path forward.

Much like the initial issues with development, getting a dealership license was not easy. At times, we were getting close to quitting the project because of the depth and complexity of the paperwork involved. Even so, we kept pushing through: focused on our goal of traveling more and retiring my mom. After almost seven months of back and forth with the appropriate agencies, we finally secured the license we needed.

It was a crucial step towards building our confidence. After all, we had sunk almost all of our money into a potential deal that seemed like it might blow up in our faces—and then with the help of the people around us, we were beginning to turn it all around.

We had paid $160,000 for all the land, and the total cost to develop the first lot with the first manufactured home was another $86,000, for a total of $246,000. Although the project had seemed like a simple way to make quick profit, it was clear that it would actually end up being a multi-year project that cost a lot more than we thought it would.

Still, even though the return might not end up being as much as we expected (because of expenses like street improvements and school taxes that would add up to roughly $130,000), we were finally starting to get our heads wrapped around the scope of the project and things were going in the right direction.

Even if we weren't seeing a return in the short term, the knowledge and confidence we had gotten from throwing ourselves into such a complex project head on only encouraged us to take on more real estate development and investing projects. We knew that we had bigger and better things ahead.

Since we realized our subdivision project would take years to come to fruition, we wanted to start another, simpler project that could pay off sooner—and the next idea was mine.

"What if we sold our condo?" I asked Yesenia one day. Although Amazon's new headquarters across from us was good for our property value, there was also an influx of new condos being built downtown and much more inventory. It meant that the high prices would only remain for a while before going down. Adding to that, the higher property value wasn't doing us much good in our day-to-day life—plus we were paying huge homeowners' association fees and were restricted from renting it on Airbnb when we traveled, which I had recently learned was a technique some investors used to supplement their income.

As I explained, we could sell our condo and use that money to buy a fixer-upper that we could live in for a while as we renovated it. Yesenia raised her eyebrows, shocked that I was suggesting something that would be such a lifestyle downgrade.

"We can look for a house with an unfinished basement," I said, "and once we finish it and rent the downstairs, the income will offset the cost of our mortgage, and we'll be able to travel more. We can even do a cash-out refinance to take some money out of the property after we improve it, and we can use *that* money to purchase the waterfront property we've been dreaming about."

After discussing it more, Yesenia and I agreed to put our condo on the market. Unfortunately, after three weeks on the market, we weren't getting any offers. Which was odd, since the average time on the market for condos in our building was only seven days.

At first, I was confused. Since I was serving as our own listing agent, I was confident I was already doing many of the right things to get the house sold—so what was going on?

I knew that the three most important things when it came to selling homes were how the house showed, how it was priced and how it was marketed. To my surprise, even though we'd had lots of client showings and had great marketing, we were not receiving any offers or much potential interest. Another condo in our complex with the exact same floor plan had gotten under contract for $10,000 less than ours, which meant that we had to drop our price as well. But even after doing that and having another showing, we still had no luck.

Feeling my frustration and uncertainty, I decided to listen to some morning affirmations on YouTube. I wanted to realign myself since my energy was feeling incredibly funky—I was excited about the future, but I was also doubtful and insecure at the same time. Yesenia and I had created so many beautiful memories in the three years we'd lived in Seattle, and leaving that behind felt like it would shake me to my core. Our condo was on the market, but we still had no place to go if it actually sold.

The affirmations began: *Everything is always working out for me*, the voice said in the video, followed by a relaxing tune. *And since everything is always working out for me, I want to define more clearly: what things would I like to be working out for me? What specific things? Not nebulous things, not general things—what specific things?*

I would like to get an offer on the condo, I thought to myself —but then, I felt a knot in my stomach. Did I *really* want to sell the condo? Having that condo had been our dream the entire time we were living there. Although we rarely used the 41st floor, which had a rooftop view, we enjoyed stunning sunset views when we had. Were we really going to give all that up to start a new adventure full of uncertainty?

While mulling it all over, something came to me: although Yesenia and I were both onboard to *list* our condo, neither of us had been certain that we really wanted to *sell* it. In a sense, I knew that it was a downgrade to move out of a luxury condo in downtown Seattle to a fixer-upper; plus, the prestige of real estate agents who sold luxury condos downtown was higher if they actually lived in the buildings, and I was just starting to break into that market.

I want to tune into the frequency of who I am and spread the joy of who I am, the voice continued. As I thought about it, I was filled with gratitude for all the people who had taught me and helped me advance.

I want to be so true to my frequency that everything I want flows to me and everything I don't want flows out, the recording continued. *What is it that I truly want?* I thought.

I tried to clear my thoughts so that I could find the answer. Part of the issue, I realized, was that my goal of selling the condo was clouded by my price point expectations and some of my nagging doubts about leaving the heart of downtown—and about finding a good deal that we could profit from after we sold.

After visualizing different scenarios and determining which one of them *felt* best, I came to a realization: selling the condo would be the scariest journey, but also potentially the most rewarding. *I'm ready to let go of this*, I thought. *I'm ready to sell this condo.* Finally, the recording stopped, and I opened my eyes to make my morning coffee.

Moments later, I saw that I had a text from an agent who had shown the condo to a client several weeks prior, before the client backed out:

Hey Carla, hope you're doing well. My client changed her mind about moving into another building, and we're submitting an offer on your condo. You should have it in your inbox shortly.

What the heck!? I thought. Getting an offer right after my visualization meditation was either pure coincidence or I had truly tapped into a powerful force in the universe—and I chose to believe it was the latter.

We accepted the offer, and a month later, in August, we sold our condo and placed all of our things in a storage unit. We found a temporary apartment an hour outside the city that was only 369 square feet, while we continued our search for a good fixer-upper.

I soon realized that finding juicy deals like the ones people talked about in investing classes and meetups was not easy. More experienced investors tended to scoop these up quickly, but we weren't about to give up. Since we had such a long commute, both of us started working from home. To maximize the space, I converted our bedroom's walk-in closet into an office, while Yesenia made her calls in the other room at the tiny kitchen table.

I was feeling more pressure than ever to find the elusive deal that I had sold Yesenia on. After another month of searching, we finally found one. It was a house that had been built in 1927 that was almost in its original state, except for the kitchen, which had been renovated at some point in the 60s. It was priced at $650,000.

After a house inspection and a meeting with several contractors, we determined that we would need to spend roughly $250,000 to renovate the house and finish the basement, adding two bedrooms and a bathroom. After all the renovations, the total project cost would be $900,000—but the after-repair value (ARV) would be $1.1 million, according to comparable sales. It meant that we stood to earn $200,000 in equity, and we could pull part of that equity out after refinancing the home and use it as a down payment on a lakefront property.

Once I'd worked out the math, I invited Chris down to see the house, and he agreed it had great potential. Together, we applied the 80 percent rule, which investors use as a guideline to determine if a house is a good buy.

The rule stated that you should only pay 80 percent of the ARV minus repair costs for a house, if you wanted the numbers to work in your favor. In this case, it meant that we shouldn't pay more than $630,000. With that in mind, Yesenia and I made an offer for $627,000. Fortunately, the owner accepted.

We used a hard money loan to finance the house, which required us to put down 15 percent of the total project cost, including renovations, as a down payment. The total came to $135,000—which was exactly the amount we had left from the sale of our condo after paying for the HELOC we had used to invest in our first project.

The entire renovation process took us four months, including finishing the basement to add a mother-in-law suite, with two bedrooms and a bathroom. Although Yesenia had initially been determined to avoid moving into a house while it was being renovated (so that we didn't end up getting divorced, she said), we did it anyway—and it ended up being worth it, because the deal was even better than we anticipated.

After renovations, we had increased the value of the property by 20 percent, or $223,000. We were putting the finishing touches on the basement in March of 2020, when we turned on the news and felt a sense of dread: Covid had come to the United States. We were nervous that it would have a brutal effect on the lending industry and the housing market, and particularly what it would do to Airbnb rentals.

Given how serious the news was and what was going on in the world, I was almost embarrassed to post our new Airbnb on social media. *This is the worst timing ever*, I thought. *Nobody is going to want to travel.* Fortunately, the worrying was unfounded because shortly after, we got a message from a traveling nurse who wanted to book the property for three months. As I saw in the early months of the pandemic, a lot of work was becoming remote—and because people had the freedom to work from home, they were choosing to travel more. The short-term rental market was booming.

With the renovations completed, we did a cash-out refinance on our property to take out the same $135,000 we had just used for the down payment and were ready to repeat the process with another property, just as planned.

The formula had worked, and we were ready to look for our lakefront vacation home!

Then I pulled out the statement I had written earlier in the year:

By the 31st of December, 2020, I will have in my possession a total amount of $250,000.

I couldn't help but smile. Between my commissions and the equity we were able to pull out of our renovation, we *did* have that amount. In one year, we had gone from a net worth of $135,000 to a net worth of $302,000—for a project that had only taken four months! Moreover, the amount we'd earned from increasing the equity on our house was *twice* what I'd earned in commissions my first year in real estate, when I was cold-calling people as often as I could.

As I was thinking it over, a thought popped into my head like a bubble rising through water: *You have to be clear in order to receive. Ask, and it shall be given.*

Reflecting on everything I'd learned from my reading and courses, it was clear how powerful the advice I'd been following was—particularly the idea of the Circle of Five. When I was living in the Tri-Cities, my circle of five and my environment in general had felt limited. Since I had moved to Seattle, my circle of five had changed completely. In it were Thatch, Adriana, Yesenia, Chris and Jan—all of them positive, motivated and growth-minded individuals who wanted to help themselves and each other flourish. On top of that, we also had Yesenia's extended family, who offered their love and support and were like another circle of five all on their own.

From my first year to the second, my real estate business and dealings grew about 50 percent using everything I'd learned—but from year two to year three, they had grown 300 percent! I knew what Yesenia and I had already accomplished was only the beginning. We were going to build a multi-million dollar rental portfolio and live the life of our dreams.

14

THE VORTEX

"As above, so below; as within, so without; as the universe, so the soul."

—HERMES TRISMEGISTUS

With the success of our first house flip behind us, Yesenia and I were filled with confidence—but in the back of my mind, I still had doubts about the L&I investigation that I knew was ongoing. It had been about a year since I'd hired my attorney on retainer, and it was almost time to check in about next steps. To my surprise, I got a check in the mail with a letter attached:

Carla—

I would have expected to hear from the investigators by now. Since it's been over a year, I don't know if the

*investigation is even still ongoing. As a result, I'm
returning your deposit. Cheers,*

Jim Frush

Feeling relief that maybe everything would work out after
all, and following Jim's advice to continue living a "normal life,"
we were ready to take the money we'd made from our first flip
to start looking for affordable lake houses on Lake Roesiger,
within an hour's drive of Seattle.

Even though we'd made a rule to not let our emotions run
the process while we searched, it was difficult at times because
we kept getting outbid—in one instance by as much as
$150,000. All the same, we forced ourselves to stick to our
numbers and not to get caught up in any bad deals.

Our profit goal on whatever home we moved into next
would have to be at least $250,000, since we knew now what
was possible with patience and dedication. Finally, after seeing
at least seven different houses that we loved and put offers on,
Yesenia found a lakehouse online priced at a reasonable
$650,000, that had been on the market for 13 days.

We were both in shock, because it was June—the prime
time to sell a waterfront property. Most of the places we were
seeing were under contract within a couple of days, and sometimes even within a few hours! I did some quick math: like our
first flip, the house was listed for $650,000 and the repairs
would cost around $250,000. Once again, Yesenia and I could
use our $125,000 to finance the entire project—and if I had
analyzed the numbers correctly, we stood to make another
$250,000 in equity when all was said and done. Though it was
a similar deal as our first flip, this time there would be a big
difference: there was no way we would live in it while it was
being renovated, as that had been hard enough the first time.

"Something has to be very wrong with this place," I said. Yesenia nodded.

"It seems almost too good to be true," she conceded, "but it won't hurt to check it out." Since it was 7 am on Sunday morning when we found the listing, we kept excitedly looking at all the pictures and waited until 9 am, when it seemed more reasonable to call the agent. Between the purchase price and the money we would need to make it livable, it seemed like a great deal and we were excited to schedule a showing—until the agent dampened our enthusiasm.

"If you don't have a million dollars cash, don't even bother coming to see the house," he said flatly. "It's falling apart. The owner bought it 13 years ago with the intent of fixing it but he never did. This one is a complete teardown."

Regardless of what the realtor had said, we went to go see the property with our home inspector and our team of contractors. As soon as my inspector saw it, he stopped outside.

"Let me save you the inspection money," he said. "I think the agent is right—the house is definitely a teardown. Between rebuilding it and the retaining walls it'll need, a million dollars sounds about right. Just pay me for my gas now and let's call it quits." Since we'd already been looking at potential properties, he'd gotten to know me well and he recognized the look I was giving him—the one that said I wasn't going to take no for an answer. Before I could even say anything, he spoke again.

"Okay, fine," he said. "We'll look inside the house and go from there." Getting to the door of the house felt like going on a hike, since the yard and the path were covered in tall weeds, with the house set beyond, wrapped in ivy. The most important thing we needed to check was if the foundation was good, but it was difficult to access because decks had fallen off of the house and were obstructing the way.

Fortunately, one of the contractors was short enough that he was able to crawl under the debris to check.

"I think the foundation is solid," he said, to our great relief. It was all I needed to hear.

After our inspection, Yesenia and I offered $590,000 for the house, $60,000 below the asking price to account for all the risk we were taking in renovating it. To our surprise, the seller accepted our offer and didn't even counter.

We had drawn up some paperwork and during our feasibility period (where we could inspect the house more thoroughly and terminate the contract if we found anything seriously amiss, without a penalty), we hired geotechnical engineers and foundation specialists to confirm what the initial inspection had shown. Everyone confirmed that the structure of the house could be saved. It would still be a major flip, but with that good news, we were confident that we could pull it off.

After months of renovations, we had spent about $308,000. It was roughly $50,000 more than we'd anticipated, but the numbers still worked because of the leverage we'd gained from buying the house for less than the asking price. When everything was done, we had the house reappraised to see how much value we'd gain in equity. The appraiser came back telling us that the house was worth $1.179 million, meaning a $402,000 increase in equity. In just two flips in a year, our combined net worth had gone from around $136,000 to close to $700,000!

Whatever Covid-related fears we'd had were unfounded, it seemed. People were moving out of cities to bigger homes with yards, and remote workers were traveling more and renting more vacation homes. At the same time, the Fed had reduced interest rates to zero percent, and mortgage rates were as low as they had ever been historically.

Since the market was doing better than ever, I was also

growing my real estate business by representing both buyers and sellers. Though I'd grown and learned a lot since I'd started, the competition was more intense than ever.

Since I had joined the luxury real estate brand, I was constantly competing with agents who had more than 10 years in the business and who also had most of the luxury listings; one of my colleagues, for example, had just been recognized for listing the most expensive house that quarter, which cost $18 million. While I was trying to work my way into more luxury listings, my edge was volume. Most of my clients were Latino—first-time homebuyers who identified with me because I was bilingual.

I was getting in a good flow, and Yesenia's success was pushing me even further. She was always one of the top performers in her office and encouraged me to compete as well, which led to me placing in the top 10 percent of agents in the company. The next big push came after Yesenia started doing online marketing. She got a huge influx of leads from it and encouraged me to do the same.

"Online marketing is the future," Yesenia said. "I know you've been learning about print marketing and flyers in your workshops, but online video is where it's at. Why don't you try video ads on Facebook?"

I knew she was right. Real estate was a massively entrepreneurial business, as every agent had to do all their own marketing and lead generation, and it was constantly changing. It made sense that I could make more commission by investing more into promotion, even if it was uncomfortable.

Yesenia convinced me to record my first video for Facebook, and I couldn't have been more nervous.

"I can't concentrate," I said, as she stood behind the camera. My hair was done up in a messy bun, and I was self-conscious about how it looked.

"Your *chongo* looks great, babe," Yesenia insisted. "Now come on, let's do this!"

With no choice but to trust her, we finally recorded an informational video (after six or so takes). I posted it, and just as Yesenia had promised, it blew up. Interestingly enough, there were tons of comments on my messy bun just as I was afraid there would be, but people were so interested in it—some complimenting it and others making fun of it—that it was helping the video get traction.

Upon seeing how many leads and sales were resulting from that first video, I started posting online regularly. Although I wasn't sure what to post about initially, Yesenia gave me helpful advice.

"Just make videos that contribute and give value to your customers," she said. "Share some tips with them about real estate."

With that advice in mind, I started making content that showed people how to qualify for a house, how to boost their credit, how to secure financing and how to invest in real estate. My focus was always on adding value to others in order to get value back in return—and soon my viewership was growing, along with my lead list.

My mindset around life and business was feeling increasingly positive and my worries of the past were fading into the back of my mind. A friend invited us to her wedding in Mexico that fall and as we drove from the airport in Zihuatanejo to our hotel, I noticed that there were three falcons in the sky above us.

"Babe, look at that!" I said, pointing out the window. For whatever reason, the birds seemed to be escorting us to our hotel. They looked majestic and beautiful, and though I thought it was slightly strange that they followed us all the way from the airport to our hotel, I soon put it out of my mind.

The next day, Yesenia and I had called a taxi to take us somewhere in town—and again, above our taxi were three falcons, escorting us in the same exact way.

"Do you see that?" I said, this time with a little more urgency. Yesenia tipped her sunglasses back and looked out the window.

"Oh yeah," she mused. "Are those the same three falcons?" They looked the same and were flying in the same formation, but it seemed impossible. As strange as it was, I put it out of my head as a coincidence.

Yesenia and I were lying out by the hotel pool the following day, getting a tan and relaxing in the sun. And once again, I saw three falcons flying in a tight formation over the pool—only this time, they were flying much lower to the ground and seemed to be circling us. Though I could write off seeing falcons two times as a coincidence, this third time seemed like a sign.

"Look at that!" I exclaimed, pointing at the sky and nudging Yesenia. Again, she took her sunglasses off, bemused.

"You should look up what it means," she said with a chuckle, putting her sunglasses back on and sipping on her mezcal drink. With that, I took out my phone and did a Google search of just that. After skimming for a while, I found an answer on a blog about spiritual guidance. It read:

Seeing falcons is a sign of ambition, power and freedom. It can signify a sign of a rebirth when considering new opportunities; however, falcons can also signify a word of caution, that whoever sees them should remain vigilant about what lies ahead.

Reading the words carefully, I was intrigued. It was a strange omen at a time when everything was going so well, though I supposed the parts about ambition and freedom rang true. *Maybe it means that there is an opportunity ahead for me to take on even more leadership,* I thought. *I'll have to be prepared for even greater opportunities that are coming!*

And it was true, after all: I had been taking on a lot of new projects and responsibilities. We had finished renovating the basement of our house and were renting it out and we had also just completed the lake house renovation. Based on the equity we'd built from those projects, we had combined two HELOCs and put deposits on two condos in Mexico, one in Tulum and one in Holbox, where I'd proposed to Yesenia. Everything seemed to be flowing rhythmically in an upward spiral.

As with our condo in Seattle, those pre-sale condos in Mexico were still under construction—and once again, they would take roughly two years to be complete, giving us time to save money to finish paying for them. No matter what opportunities came my way, I had to remain vigilant and be open to receive them.

For the entire two weeks we were in Mexico celebrating with my friend, falcons kept appearing overhead periodically, and upon seeing them, I just smiled, choosing to believe that it was some sort of message sent from above. Though I was having a blast with our friends, I was excited to get back home and to plunge into more opportunities for growth.

The next morning after arriving home, I came down to the kitchen and made myself a cup of morning coffee, then went to the mailbox to pick up our mail. Since we'd been gone for two weeks, there was quite a lot of it, so I sat down on the living room sofa with my coffee and sorted through it, thinking of how grateful I was for my life and feeling at peace.

After rifling through a few credit card offers, magazines and other junk mail, I saw a letter from the State of Washington addressed to me that gave me pause. It was in an unmarked envelope, but it was a thick letter and was marked urgent. With my heart fluttering, I opened the letter and read what it said:

> STATE OF WASHINGTON,
> *Plaintiff,*
> V.
> CARLA C. MORENO,
> *Defendant.*
>
> *The Attorney General of Washington, in the name and authority of the State of Washington, do accuse CARLA C. MORENO of the crimes of: Theft in the Third Degree (one count) and Identity Theft in the First Degree (one count).*

Upon reading the first few lines, my stomach dropped and my heart started racing. I could only skim the rest of the document, but the main takeaway was what I feared most: the state was trying to charge me with two separate felonies, and they had pages of documentation and accounts they were planning to use against me in court.

My body was starting to turn cold and I could feel myself hyperventilating, so I put my hand on my chest and tried to calm myself down. Meanwhile, my thoughts were spiraling out of control:

Maybe I should flee to Mexico right now before they come to my house with a restraining order and throw me in jail for years. I could cut all business ties here, divest from all the active investments I have...but what about Yesenia? And what about our family?

L&I has no idea what they're talking about! I wasn't trying to deceive anybody, so much of this is just a misunderstanding...

I should just pack my bags and leave. I can't believe this is happening to me. I tried so hard to dig myself out of so many deep holes, but this time it's different. My life as I knew it is over...

I was in a state of total panic. I called Jim immediately and he confirmed how bad the situation was.

"This is worse than I thought it would be," he said. "I'll defend you, but I have to warn you upfront that it's not going to be cheap. If we end up going to trial, it'll be best if you can save around $200,000 for all the expenses you might incur. The worst-case outcome of this is years in jail and deportation, though obviously I'm going to fight as hard as I can to avoid that." Everything had been going so well that hearing this news practically gave me vertigo.

After receiving it, I kept to myself as much as I could and didn't tell anyone what was going on other than Yesenia. The only exception was getting together with a close friend to watch the 2020 presidential election.

The day after, I got another call.

"Hey Carla," my friend said. "I have some bad news, girl. I wasn't feeling one hundred percent when we had dinner together the other night, so I went to get a Covid test. I just got the results, and they're positive."

Once again, my stomach dropped. *Covid?!* I thought. *What's next?* I'd been watching the news and trying to stay informed about the pandemic, but for the most part, there was no reliable information. There were no treatments or vaccines at this time, no clear advice on what to do if you got sick and no solid guidelines as to who was most at risk. In some cases, Covid was just a very bad cold; in others, it could mean total lung failure and even death.

After getting off the phone, I called Yesenia and told her the news, explaining that we had to make an appointment at a testing site right away. We were able to make an appointment the next day, and after waiting in line with clouds rolling in overhead, we both got our noses swabbed and drove home and waited for our results. A day or so later, each of us got a notification from the testing clinic and breathed a sigh of relief: we were negative.

That was close, I thought, *especially with my birthday coming up.*

For my birthday, we took a quick weekend visit to the Tri-Cities and had a small gathering with some close friends and my mom at a friend's house. A few days later, we all started to feel very sick. One of my friends who attended the gathering confirmed it: they had gotten a Covid test and it had come back positive. It meant that everyone in attendance who was feeling sick had gotten Covid as well, including Yesenia and me.

Sure enough, soon Yesenia and I both felt aches all over our bodies and were drained of energy. On top of feeling terrible physically, there was also the guilt that my birthday had been the cause of so many of my friends getting Covid as well.

This is a nightmare, I thought. *I was already about to lose everything, but now there's a chance that me, my friends and family might die as well. I wish the earth would just open up and swallow me whole already.*

15

EGO DEATH

"He who fears he will suffer, already suffers because he fears."

—*MICHEL DE MONTAIGNE*

The week Yesenia and I had Covid found both of us collapsed in bed with body aches, fevers and coughs, barely able to move or look at the light—and I had plenty of time to ruminate on all the bad things that I was sure were coming my way. Just weeks before, I had felt myself surging upward like a bird on a warm current of air. Now, it felt like I was surging down a toilet bowl vortex of negativity.

Thankfully, both Yesenia and all of our friends recovered from Covid without any severe illness or needing to go to the emergency room—though shortly after, everything in Seattle began to shut down. Major businesses were closing their doors and all kinds of public services and utilities were changing.

People were being ordered to stay inside, socially distance and limit their exposure to the disease.

I had already made the first arrangements to defend myself against the charges coming my way, and sent Jim a hefty retainer, knowing the trouble that we faced ahead. With his help, we started sending in whatever paperwork and documentation we needed to be in compliance with the investigation and not make things worse. Eventually, we found out that my court date was set for September 2021—a full 11 months away, hanging there like a death sentence.

Instead of filling my mind with inspirational thoughts, I had sunk to the level of focusing on my defense and survival.

"The prosecutor is arguing that you billed double for your appointments," Jim explained, "and that you stole peoples' identities in order to do it."

"Things are not how they seem," I said with anguish. "It was only to keep my interpreters working until they could get certified all the way—and I never got paid more than once for any appointments!" I knew the dispute was over the vouchers I'd re-sent to L&I when they switched to the new system, but I also knew it was difficult to explain and that it looked different on the surface.

As I read through the papers, I started noticing the dates of when witnesses were interviewed and evidence was collected and got increasingly frustrated. Interpreters from the past, including Maria, had been talking to state investigators about me for a very long time—while writing encouraging comments on my Facebook posts and keeping up outward appearances of everything being fine. Likewise, Lucio had given investigators extensive evidence and testimony against me.

As the gyms closed due to the pandemic, I fell off my exercise routine—and the rest of my morning routine went along with it. I wasn't meditating in the morning anymore.

Instead, I was spending more days in my pajamas walking around the house like some disembodied entity trapped in purgatory, feeling sorry for myself and awaiting my final judgment.

As the holidays approached, Yesenia and I were still stuck inside, not visiting our families and friends, for fear of infecting anyone else. As we watched the news, we kept hearing the message of how deadly the disease was for older people, and we didn't want to risk anyone's health. Still, the isolation had us both slipping deeper into depression.

"I feel like if one more thing happens," I said on a FaceTime call with Yesenia's family, "I won't be strong enough to handle it. I feel like I have no control over anything right now. Life is so uncertain and I can't take any more."

"I know you don't want to hear this right now," Yesenia's sister Sandra said, "but you need to try to look at the positive side of life. That's what you always tell us when one of us is struggling. Now, you have to follow your own advice. You and Yesenia have one another. You have your health, you have income, you have a place to stay. Things could be a whole lot worse—and they will get a whole lot worse if you don't focus on positive thoughts."

The same day, my mom gave me virtually the same message and reminded me of the importance of spiritual strength.

"You will get through this, Carlita," she said. "Remember all the things that were helping you live the life you wanted and stay positive. The only thing you can have total control over is your own thoughts."

When the day was over, Yesenia and I looked at one another and had a mutual agreement: we couldn't go on living the way we were. We had to get back into our old, healthy routines, no matter how bleak everything around us looked. We had already wallowed in self-pity and defeat for several months. Now, it was time to restore my life force so I could start turning things around.

Over the next few weeks, I reminded myself to take a deep breath whenever I was feeling too stressed and I started meditating again in the mornings. Even though the gyms were closed, Yesenia and I decided that we still had no excuse not to exercise; in fact, we had the resources to bring the gym to us.

After clearing out some space, we ordered some used home gym equipment online, built it and set it up in our garage. I used chalk on the wall to write down my goals and a tally system for days I exercised, and what I would do in each workout. At first, thoughts of betrayal and victimization would still float into my mind—until one day, after I was lifting weights, I felt a shift.

When my workout was over, I started to journal to process what I was feeling:

When the sun is shining and the birds are chirping, it's easy to be grateful for the wonderful things in life. But it is in the midst of chaos that it is especially important to find gratitude. To take a moment and reflect, or to ask, "What is this trying to teach me?"

When you sow victimization, you reap weakness. When you sow lies, you reap blame and project onto others hate. Because sometimes it's easier to blame others than to take responsibility for our own fate.

But when you sow extreme ownership in your actions, when you sow love and kindness, magic and harmony begin to happen. At the end, chaos recedes, truth prevails and the lesson remains.

I put my pen down. *I need to take my own responsibility for this situation,* I thought. *I can't blame anyone else. It was my decision to use other interpreters' provider numbers without their permission and I always knew I shouldn't have. This is my fault. Even if some of what the prosecutors are saying isn't true, I have to accept responsibility for what I did and face it head-on.*

Along with exercise and meditation, I started other spiritual practices to be as positive as I could. In the mornings, I burned Palo Santo in our house to ward off negativity and I started writing down positive affirmations in my journal again. I knew I needed to be as mentally strong as possible for my court date in September by keeping up my morning routines, even when I didn't want to.

I also started reading self-development books again—and in the middle of a book, one of the lines jumped out at me:

Things don't happen to you, they happen for you.

As hard as I'd been trying to let go of my negativity, it wasn't until I read those words that I could fully make the change. I had to fully let go of whatever anger and resentment I had, no matter how hard it would be, because holding onto it would only attract more negativity into my life and keep me stuck in the same cycle.

Things were starting to become more clear. I had been growing fast with no grounding or direction. Having the ability to create my own path was a skill that had served me tremendously as an entrepreneur, but the misuse of those same skills had gotten me in trouble as I crossed the grey line. I had touched rock bottom for a reason: it was time to establish healthy new rules and clear boundaries for growth with harmonious balance.

With this new mentality in place, I understood that this situation was a must—it was a necessary checkpoint to ensure a better quality of myself. Strangely, although I felt like I was in the center of a supermassive black hole, I also sensed that in due time, I would eventually see the light.

About a month before I was due in court, the first articles starting appearing online about my upcoming court date, all of them with shocking headlines:

Former Tri-Cities business owner stole $43K from State

Pasco business owner charged with defrauding state L&I

Washington woman defends against fraud charges found by L&I

As the articles appeared online, friends and family members started forwarding them to me along with concerned messages:

Wanted to make sure you saw this—is everything okay?

So sorry you're going through this—thinking of you and Yes.

Stay strong!

With court coming up, I knew I faced severe consequences —I could be forced back to Mexico after going to jail for a long time. Still, seeing those headlines and reading those articles, I realized that none of those things had actually been my greatest fear throughout the year.

Instead, my greatest fear had come true, and it was staring me in the face: *What are people going to think of me?*

I had spent so long setting boundaries with my family,

coming out of the closet and trying to live my life as a proud queer woman. I had worked hard to set myself up financially, to push beyond my limits and to grow. Yesenia and I had achieved our goal of being millionaires and were about to close on two condos in Mexico—but none of that would matter if I lost all of my freedom.

Because of my mistakes, my reputation was going to be destroyed. Now, whenever someone searched my name, they would see accusations that I was a thief and a bad person who allegedly only became successful by cheating others. And the entire situation was incredibly unfair to Yesenia. There was no reason that she should suffer because of decisions I made that didn't even involve her.

As I read through the articles, I felt tears in my eyes. My life was over. What would happen to my mom's reputation now that she was the mother of a criminal? What would people say about my wife at work? How would anyone look at me in a positive light ever again? Inside I felt like I was dying—until I had a realization.

Ever since I'd found out about the investigation, I'd been feeling uncertain, paranoid and ashamed, even as I tried to live a normal life. Now, the one thing I had feared the most for nearly five years had happened to me—and I was still alive. I cared so much about my reputation being damaged, but there were still people who truly knew me, supported me and would be there for me in my worst times. Perhaps most important of all, there were still people who believed my version of the story.

Although the comments on the articles were full of negative, hateful words, they were all strangers who didn't know me. The direct messages I received were filled with kind, loving words from close friends and family wishing me well, supporting me and encouraging me not to lose hope.

"No matter what happens," Yesenia said one evening,

"we're going to get through this together. Even if it means fleeing to Mexico." We both laughed a little. Though she was just trying to lighten the mood, I knew on some level she was serious. She was willing to go to the end of the world with me and to stand by my side in spite of everything.

No matter what the outcome is, I thought, *having this woman by my side is worth more than its weight in gold.*

After carefully reviewing all the evidence against me and building a defense, Jim met and negotiated with the prosecution to arrive at a plea deal for a more favorable sentence (and hopefully to avoid jail time). Jim and the prosecution team were volleying emails back and forth, adjusting the wording on various demands, until it seemed they had settled on something everyone could agree to.

In exchange for pleading guilty, the prosecution would adjust my charges to a gross misdemeanor of theft in the third degree. I would perform 30 days of community service. The last issue that remained was the maximum recommended sentence, and the wording of it was critical.

Though Jim and the prosecution were mostly in agreement, we were adamant that the maximum recommended sentence be 180 days in jail. It was imperative for immigration reasons, because if I'd been given a 365-day maximum sentence as the prosecution originally wanted, it would likely mean an automatic deportation. Without giving up any of our leverage, Jim did his best to stress how important the issue was; unfortunately, it was the one thing left unresolved when it was time for our hearing.

When the day finally came, I met Jim outside the courthouse so we could enter together.

"There won't be any big surprises ahead, right Jim?" I asked him as we walked through the halls.

"No," he replied. "It's pretty straightforward and you've

already seen all the evidence they're planning to present. You'll plead guilty to the charges, pay the restitution and get 30 days of community service." Shortly after we sat down and reviewed everything together one last time, court was officially in session.

"Mrs. Moreno," the judge said. "You have been accused of defrauding the Department of Labor and Industries during the months of August through October, 2015." My heart started beating faster. "The maximum sentence for this crime is 365 days, and counsel's recommendation is 30 days suspended." Hearing this, I turned to Jim with a little uncertainty, but he made a hand gesture that I should remain calm. My heart was beating so loud that I could hear it in my head, as the judge finished the first part of his address and looked at me.

"Mrs. Moreno, please stand up," he said. Blood was rushing into my brain so fast that I felt like my soul was going to leave my body. Through all my adrenaline and fear, the judge's voice sounded like it was distorted.

"How do you plead to the charges you've been accused of?" he asked.

"Guilty, Your Honor," I said finally, my whole body shaking. He nodded. The judge was about to read the sentence when the prosecutor stood up to address the court.

"Before sentencing, Your Honor," the prosecutor said, "I would like to add a statement."

"Go ahead, Mrs. Sierra," the judge replied.

"Your Honor," she said as she stood up. "This plea agreement was not reached easily, and the damage in this matter was substantial. The parties do agree that a suspended sentence of 30 days is fine. The State wants to point out, however, that Mrs. Moreno has already received substantial benefit from this plea agreement, and based on the nature and severity of the case and monetary loss, our recommendation is that you impose the maximum sentence of 365 days." Hearing her words made my whole body turn cold.

"The Department of Labor and Industries is not the only affected party here," the prosecutor continued. "Carla Moreno used the names and provider numbers of certified interpreters who no longer worked for her to bill for appointments covered by non-certified interpreters. They didn't know she was using their numbers to bill for those appointments until an L&I investigator notified them. Some of the interpreters who have been following this case were not happy with this resolution and feel like Mrs. Moreno is getting off too easy. In fact, one of them told me it felt like a slap in the face."

"Actually," she continued, "I would like to take just a couple of minutes to ask if there are any interpreters present in the courtroom whose names were used who would wish to speak to the court?" As she said it, my stomach dropped. *She brought witnesses?*

"Jim," I whispered, "I thought this was just a hearing, not a trial. How can she call witnesses and why don't we have any?" Jim looked furious.

"The prosecutor didn't mention anything about this but technically they're not people testifying," he replied in frustration. "She's trying to throw a curveball at us."

I turned behind me where my mom, my friend Krystal, Yesenia and her sisters were sitting. Although they all looked as pale and distressed as I did, the fact that they were there gave me some comfort and strength.

"Oh! I see we do have some interpreters who are joining us virtually," the prosecutor said, pretending it was a surprise as she pointed to a large screen next to the judge's stand. My heart dropped when I saw two names on the screen: Lucio and Maria.

"Hello, Your Honor," Maria's voice crackled through the

screen. Though I could hear her voice, her face was hidden. "I just want to say: the fraud she committed against this state agency is appalling to me. This plea agreement is disgraceful!" At that, she began to cry. "It makes me sick to my stomach that there are people trying to live their life in an ethical way, while she is deliberately orchestrating something like this. I would appreciate it if you would take a closer look at her criminal history, Your Honor." With that, she started crying harder than before.

My criminal history? I thought, confused. *What is she talking about?* Maria and I barely knew each other, and as far as I knew, I had never done her wrong, other than by using her name to change one voucher—so why was she crying like I had killed her cat? A moment later, Maria's voice disappeared and Lucio's appeared on the speaker.

"Hello, Your Honor," he said. "I'd like to read a statement." After a brief pause to prepare himself, he continued.

"I would like to say that I believe that Carla knew exactly what she was doing," he said. "I knew there were irregular things going on, which I found out about later—and I even tried to help her initially, because we were friends at the time. But I can say for a fact that I witnessed forms being filled out under my name, which were sent out when I was no longer working for her. It really bothers me that she went as far as using my information without my consent."

After the additional testimony, the prosecutor spoke again.

"Your Honor," she said, "I just ask the court to focus on the underlying facts of this case. Mrs. Moreno did not just defraud the Department of Labor and Industries, she defrauded her own community, her friends and hard-working people who tried to follow the rules. Again, we ask the court to impose 365 days."

"Mrs. Sierra," the judge replied. "I understand that these

interpreters feel personally violated, but why do you see a benefit in the longer suspended sentence, if the defendant is only going to serve 30 days and not the entire sentence?"

Frozen, I turned to Jim.

"What does this mean?" I asked him with my heart pounding. "Will I have to serve the entire year in jail?"

"Hold on," he whispered, putting his hand on my shoulder again as the prosecutor and judge finished their discussion.

"Your Honor, the concern is that if the state does not impose the maximum sentence, Mrs. Moreno will again be benefiting," the prosecutor said. "We feel like she should be given the same sentence as any other criminal, and 365 days is typically the sentence imposed."

"She is only going to serve a total of 30 days, so it is pointless to impose a maximum sentence," the judge said with frustration in his voice. "It sounds to me that you want to add extra punishment because of the defendant's immigration status."

"Certainly not, Your Honor," the prosecutor replied nervously.

"Mrs. Moreno," the judge continued, turning again to me, "the court is going to find you guilty of theft in the third degree. You will have to pay the full restitution to the Department of Labor and Industries of $43,000." After a moment of silence, he continued. "The court is going to order you to serve 179 days, with 149 suspended. The court will have you serve 10 of those days in jail, and the remaining 20 days on electronic home monitoring."

With a bang of his gavel, our hearing was over. I was still scared about jail, but at the very least, the sentence wasn't going to result in immediate deportation. Then again, there was still the risk that immigration could come and pull me out of my cell in the middle of the night.

16

DARKNESS AND LIGHT

"A life spent making mistakes is not only more honorable, but more useful than a life spent doing nothing."

—GEORGE BERNARD SHAW

"Moreno! Grab your stuff!" the guard shouted as he opened the door. "We're moving you to another cell with the other inmates. You can make your phone call from there."

A ray of sunlight came through the cell as the guard opened the door, illuminating the otherwise dark room. It was like heaven itself was opening up in front of me.

"What time is it? How long have I been here for?" I asked him, as I dried my tears.

"It's 5 pm," he replied. "You've been here for 24 hours." *It might have only been 24 hours,* I thought, *but it feels like an eternity.*

I thought of Dante's purgatory as the officer walked me

through the labyrinthine hallways. Finally, we approached a larger cell consisting of two adjacent rooms and a small corridor with exposed toilets and showers.

"Do you take showers?" one of the inmates shouted at me, staring at me with threatening eyes as I passed in front of her. She was short, chubby and didn't have any teeth.

"Um, y-yes," I answered, "I do." *I hope that was the right answer*, I thought.

"Okay," the inmate replied, "then you can share this room with me and Boston." She pointed at the room where a tall Black inmate with long braided hair was standing next to the door. She shifted her hips from side to side, making her braids dance and smiled, revealing a golden tooth shining in her mouth.

"You can also call me G," Boston said, with a smirk on her face.

"That one over there doesn't take showers and she fucking stinks!" the first inmate said, pointing at another woman with greasy red hair who was face down in her bed, curled in the fetal position and covered in sweat. "That's Red. She's in that other room by herself. Trust me, you don't want to be there."

"Oh, okay. Thank you," I said, placing my mattress and blanket on an empty metal bed frame, grateful to be in a room with people who *did* take showers.

"She seems scary, but she's a sweetheart," whispered Boston, gesturing at the first inmate. "Her name's Brenda. She looks like she's 70 but she's only 43. Drugs." She shook her head in disapproval.

"Oh shut up, Boston!" yelled Brenda from across the room. "You're the one that sells them!"

"Yeah, but I *only* sell them," Boston yelled back, pointing her finger to her head to allude to how smart she was. "I don't consume them."

"Yes you do! Don't fucking lie! I saw you doing blues the other day at the park with JJ!" *What are blues?* I thought to myself.

"You know JJ?" Brenda asked me, snapping me out of my thoughts.

"No, I don't," I replied.

"Bitch, you don't know what you're talking about," Boston yelled at Brenda, clearly still mad about the drug conversation. "Don't make me stab you again!"

"Don't you dare go there again, G," Brenda growled. "I'll fuck you up this time around!" She turned to me and unbuttoned part of her jumpsuit, showing me her belly with several marks on it. "This bitch stabbed me two years ago," she explained to me, pointing at herself. "I still have the scars."

"Only because you snitched, you motherfucker," Boston said. "Remember: snitches get stitches." I gulped. *Fuck,* I thought.

After a little back and forth, they eventually both agreed that the stabbing incident had been a misunderstanding, and they were willing to let it go since it had been so long ago—and after all, Brenda still needed Boston to be her supplier.

"Anyway," Boston said, throwing her arm around Brenda and turning my way, "welcome to the dungeon!" All I could think was to run to the phone and call my wife. I needed to hear her voice—but before I could, Boston was interrogating me again.

"What charges are you here for?" she asked.

"It's complicated," I replied. "Gross misdemeanor for allegedly defrauding the Department of Labor and Industries."

"You faked getting hurt and got money from 'em or what?" Brenda asked with a sinister laugh, revealing her toothless gums.

"No," I replied. "I used to own an interpreting agency. We

provided interpreting services for people who got injured at work, and we billed L&I so they could pay us for those appointments. Five years ago, an investigation began against me for supposedly double-billing them."

"How much money did you steal?" Brenda asked.

"According to them, $43,000," I replied.

"Oh, *daaang*," Boston said, pointing at me. "We got a smart one over here!"

"Well, I did *bill* twice," I said defensively, "but I didn't get *paid* twice!"

"Well, why did you bill twice?" Boston asked.

I took a breath to try to explain: every electronic bill I sent had to be backed by a faxed, physical form as proof that the appointment had occurred. However, I had sent hundreds of bills on old forms that L&I had stopped accepting, so all of those were denied and needed to be re-sent on new forms. Instead of having my interpreters go back to clinics to get new forms to submit, I asked my assistant to transfer the information from the old forms onto new ones and fax them again.

"What was so wrong about that?" Boston asked, confused.

"Copying the forms that way meant also copying over the signatures," I replied.

"Couldn't you prove that you didn't get paid twice?"

"Yes," I said wearily, "but it would have involved going to trial, which is very expensive. And either way, I would've been in trouble for the signatures."

"So how many days are you in here for?" she asked.

"Ten days," I replied sadly.

"Oh girl, that's nothing!" Boston said loudly. "I'm here for nine months."

"And three for me," Brenda yelled from across the room, "but I don't want to be out on the streets in January when it's freezing. I'm gonna have to figure out a way to come back or stay—at least it's warm here and I have food."

I couldn't believe what I was hearing—she wanted to stay for *more* time? All I could think about was how quickly I could get out of there. *Life is a paradox*, I thought wryly. After a moment, the sound of keys clinking together interrupted us, as an officer opened the cell.

"Moreno!" he boomed. The guard was wheeling up a cart of books. "Ask and you shall receive," he said. The three of us ran up to pick through the offerings, but by the time I got up there, there was only one left: *The Biography of Bill Cosby*.

"Ugh," I said, disappointed. "I don't want to read the biography of a guy who raped kids."

"What are you talking about?" Brenda asked. "He just got off. It was all over the news!"

"Girl, you shouldn't be so quick to judge," Boston added. "Sometimes we end up here for doing shit, but other times we end up here just because people think we did shit and we actually didn't."

"Yeah," Brenda said, "like the first time I ended up in jail in Arizona. They caught me with a small bag of weed and gave me two years in prison. That shit ruined my entire life—and it wasn't even mine, it was my stupid boyfriend's."

"They arrested me just because I wanted to see my kids," said Red, who had finally gotten out of bed to use the toilet.

"My in-laws called the police and charged me with trespassing into their home," Red said. "I was just in the garage, arguing with my baby daddy."

I thought it over. Though I was *pretty* sure Bill Cosby was guilty, I heard their point. I thought of what Jim had said to me once while we were preparing for court: *It's not the truth that matters, Carla. It's only what people perceive the truth to be.*

I was finally able to get my phone call and talk to my wife

before going to bed and just hearing her voice soothed me. It was almost like I could feel her embrace, despite the distance between us, and I felt more calm. We talked for about half an hour, until the guards yelled that it was time for bed.

Boston gave me one of the four mattresses that she had piled up to help with the stiffness of her metal bed, and Brenda gave me two of the seven blankets she was using to keep herself warm.

"The more you're here, the more you learn the tricks," Brenda said, winking at me. As the lights went off, and I sat in the dungeon-like darkness, I was surprised to find myself feeling so safe. I couldn't get Boston's words out of my head about judging other people, so I kept repeating them over and over until I fell asleep.

That night, I had the strangest dream.

I was inside a bright, round room, with a lit candle set in the middle, next to where I was standing. That small candle illuminated the entire space, all the way to the white walls. As I walked farther from the center of the room and away from the light, my black shadow got bigger and bigger until I was so close to the wall that I could touch it. Now, the white wall was completely covered by my black shadow.

When I walked back towards the center, the shadow would get smaller and smaller, until the entire room was back in light and harmony—though I hadn't appreciated the light or noticed my shadow at all until I walked away from the center in the first place.

I woke up in the middle of the night and knew I wouldn't be able to go back to sleep easily. So, I grabbed a piece of paper and a pen that I saw next to Boston (*I'll replace it later*, I thought) and began to write.

Franklin County Jail, Pasco (Day Two in Jail)

My interpretation of today's crazy dream:
I was inside a room with darkness and light, repre-
senting two forces—we sometimes call them good and
bad, positive and negative or black and white. Another
way to think of these two forces is our purpose and
mission.

If our mission is to learn how to navigate through life
and find happiness, then the purpose will come in and
bring us lessons, so we can make mistakes and learn. If
the purpose was to learn, then the mission was accom-
plished. So instead of asking, why is this happening to
me? We can ask: what is this trying to teach me?

Only by understanding that there is a purpose, can we
uncover the lesson hiding within. And only by under-
standing the lesson and moving back to the illuminated
center, do we see that the darkness was just a projection
of the light, created by our own shadow.

What we call problems are just lessons seen from
different perspectives, waiting for us to uncover their
meaning. Without darkness, there's no light; it's just a
matter of finding the balance between them and under-
standing that it is not what happens to us that matters,
but rather the meaning we give to each situation.

I put my pen down. Like my dream had shown me, I had
moved away from the light. I realized that my ego and my reputation had completely died in the courtroom. In a sense, I had
forfeited my old mission, whatever that had been.

Now, it was time to find a new one and to open myself up again to my purpose—my real purpose. It was time to find my way back to the light again.

———

"Ladies! Breakfast!" shouted the guard, waking us all up, as he placed the brown lunch bags on the floor.

I crawled out of bed, rubbing my eyes to view the familiar sight: a boiled egg, an apple and a piece of unappealing bread.

"It's always the same, girl," Boston said from her bed next to me, noticing my disappointment.

"Yeah," Brenda added, "and I don't know how they think I'm supposed to eat the apple." With that, she opened her mouth wide to show me her gums once again.

"I can give you my bread if you want," I offered.

"You would do that for me?" she asked. Her eyes were wide open and she had a huge smile. It was as if I were giving candy to a little kid.

"Of course!" I said. *Wow*, I thought. *Here I am being a brat about the same bread that just made Brenda's day.*

With that, she grabbed my bread and stuffed the whole piece in her mouth at once.

"I can fit more in there since I have no teeth," she said, smiling.

"Brenda, stop doing that!" Boston yelled. "You're gonna choke, and it looks disgusting!"

"Leave me alone," Brenda yelled back, muffled by bread. "Sometimes I go days without eating, so I have to make it up when I can."

"Ain't nobody gonna steal your food in here, fool," Boston replied, "and especially not your bread. That shit looks nasty! You're gonna get even fatter if you keep eating that shit."

"But it's sooo good," she replied, still savoring it.

Brenda's kind, child-like energy was contagious, as she savored our jail food like it was a French delicacy. I wondered if I had ever passed her on the streets of downtown Pasco without noticing her. Yes, she was a drug addict and a criminal, but I wondered what her story was and how we'd ended up in the same room together.

Once Brenda finished eating, she reached under her bed and grabbed a nearly empty bottle of shampoo and a worn out bar of soap, along with some roll-on deodorant and a small ripped towel she used as a shower scrub.

"Here," she said, smiling as she proudly handed the items over to me. "You're kind to me, so I'll be kind to you. You can use my stuff if you want to shower until you can buy your own from the commissary."

"Thank you, Brenda," I replied, warmed by the gift. Something inside me had shattered the day I arrived at that jail, but I was starting to realize there were still things to be grateful for. In a sense, I was starting to revisit the world with new eyes.

I took a shower with Brenda's shampoo, changed back into my jumpsuit and read the biography of Bill Cosby on my bed for a few hours until the guard came back again.

"Grab your stuff, ladies, we're going upstairs!" Officer Bailey shouted. The inmates all scurried and shouted with excitement; clearly, everyone was thrilled.

"What's upstairs?" I asked, confused.

"The light!" replied Red with enthusiasm, looking up and stretching her hands out like she was reaching for the sun.

"They're transferring us to a bigger area that has a big skylight," Boston clarified.

"Yeah, it's so depressing in this dark dungeon," Brenda added. "Plus, upstairs is where the rest of the female inmates are!" She clapped her hands in excitement.

"How cool would it be if my mom was up there?" Red added, joining Brenda in her excitement by rubbing her own hands together. *Her mom?* I thought.

"Is there a chance you might find her there?" I asked.

"She's usually here," she replied. "Well, sometimes she's at the one in Kennewick." I knew Kennewick was the next town over, but beyond that, I was still confused.

The guards took us upstairs and as promised, the room was very bright—so bright that it took my eyes a moment to adjust. As we stepped into the large, open cell, two inmates popped out of their rooms and ran to see who was coming.

"Rosa Alba!" exclaimed Boston, as she reached out to hug an older inmate. Like Brenda, she seemed like she was in her 40s, but she also seemed much older because she had no teeth. She was also short and chubby, with a very deep voice and short copper hair.

"What's up, I'm Brie," the younger of the two inmates said to us. She seemed to be in her 20s and had light skin, long black hair fixed in two braids and a charismatic attitude.

"Is it just the two of you here?" asked Red.

"Yeah," said Brie. "I'm glad they brought you guys up here! It has been just the two of us by ourselves for the last couple of weeks."

I scanned the area as the girls began to chat and move around. It had seven small cells, each of which barely had enough space for a bunk bed. Outside in the main area were two large tables directly beneath the skylight, and on the right side of the room located near the exposed toilets and showers. *Can't blame Red for not wanting to shower much,* I thought.

I had identified a room I liked and was walking over to place my mattress and blankets inside when Boston asked me to come over into Rosa Alba's cell, where all the inmates were congregating with suspicion. *Oh God,* I thought, *how do I tell her that I don't want drugs without pissing her off?*

"Yes?" I said, with my voice shaking as I stood by the door.

"You want some coffee lines?" Brie asked, as she sniffed something up her nose. *Coffee lines?* I thought. *Literally coffee?*

"What is that?" I asked.

"Coffee!" Brie replied, as she lifted up a jar of Nescafe.

"Why not just drink it?" I genuinely asked.

"Because it goes through your system much faster when you sniff it," Brie explained, "and you feel a rush like it was a drug!" *Well technically,* I thought, *a drug is any substance that has a psychological effect when introduced into the body, regardless of how it's introduced, so I'm not even going to judge.*

"Do it! Do it! Do it!" all the inmates chanted at me at the same time.

Shoot, I thought. *Do I sniff coffee up my nose to fit in, or do I tell them no and run the risk of potentially offending them? What if they don't like me anymore?* After a few seconds of deliberation, I thought that when in doubt, it was best to just be yourself.

"No! I don't want to sniff coffee up my nose! You guys are crazy!" I replied finally, while laughing. "But could I have my portion and drink it instead? I've been dying for a cup of coffee since I got here."

"You're seriously not gonna try it?" Boston asked in a bit of a demanding voice.

"No, I just don't want to have it quickly and all at once, when I can instead enjoy it slowly with every sip," I said, still smiling.

"You have a point there," Boston agreed, handing me her mug. "You can use mine for now until your commissary comes in. Just let the shower run for a couple minutes so it warms up before you grab the water."

I proceeded to make myself a coffee with the not-so-warm water from the shower, took it to my new, smaller cot and lay on the bottom bed. Boston followed me with her stuff.

"Nuh-uh, girl," Boston said, shaking her head in disapproval. "The bottom one is mine. Yours is the one on top."

Although there were enough rooms for each of us to have our own, everyone decided to share bunk beds with someone else to have a little company. Like them, I also felt the need to not be alone at night—even if Boston snored like a lion.

That night, I could see a beautiful full moon through the skylight. The whiteness of it reflected on the same trees that looked green and vibrant earlier with the sunshine; now, in the pale moonlight, they looked muted, ominous and full of the critters of the night—though still beautiful.

There is beauty in darkness, just as there is in light, I thought.

I had always heard that you only truly came to life through an experience that felt like death. Even in the short time I had been in jail, I felt parts of my old self falling away, and new perspectives coming to the surface. I was willing to do some self-reflection with an open mind and find out what light could come out of it.

17

REBIRTH

"Life is like riding a bicycle. To keep your balance, you must keep moving."

—*ALBERT EINSTEIN*

My 10-day sentence passed quickly, and by the time release day finally came, Boston and Brenda felt like friends that I was sad to be leaving behind. Somehow, I had made it through my jail time safe and without immigration coming for me, despite my paranoia that it could happen at any moment.

I was set to be released at 5 pm and was counting down the minutes. As 5 pm came and went, and the clock approached 5:30 pm, I could feel the anxiety rising in my chest. *What if there's an order from immigration to hold me out so they can transfer me to the deportation center?* I thought.

After waiting for as long as I could, I thought about hitting the "forbidden button" in our cell—which communicated directly with officers, in the case of an extreme emergency. Still, this felt like it qualified. With Boston and Brenda's encouragement, I finally found the courage to hit the button and was on the intercom with an officer.

"Excuse me, officer, I was supposed to get out at 5 pm," I said nervously. "Do you know what's the hold up?"

"They're doing some stuff to your file," the officer said, his voice crackling through the speaker. "Someone should be coming to get you shortly." It was so vague that it sounded like an excuse to buy time. Still, I had no choice but to wait and try to avoid despair.

Finally, around 6 pm, I saw the guard walking down the hall to get me. *Finally*, I thought. As he approached, I turned to say my goodbyes to Boston and Brenda.

"I'm keeping your contact," Boston said. "I'm getting transferred to prison after this, but I'm going to call you when I'm out of here. I want to buy a house!"

"And I want details about when the shaman is coming back in town," Brenda added—while they had been talking about their experiences with drugs, I told them about the ayahuasca experience I'd had with Yesenia and Tanya. "Maybe she can help me kick these blues."

Though it sounded like she wanted a cure for depression, I now knew that "blues" meant pain pills laced with fentanyl.

"Thank you both for everything," I said finally.

With that, the guard marched me back through the labyrinth of doom and flung the front doors open. I squinted, as my eyes struggled to adjust to the shining sun. Then I saw Yesenia silhouetted in front of the sunset, waiting for me with a bouquet of red roses.

I ran to her, kissed her and gave her a big hug, squeezing her tightly and feeling more grateful for her than ever.

"Come on," she said, opening the car door for me. "Everyone is waiting for you."

"Who is everyone?" I asked.

"You'll see," she said with a smile.

After driving through the city, we pulled up in front of her sister's house, where her parents, my mom and all of her sisters, their husbands and kids were waiting for me. Seeing everyone there made my heart feel ready to burst, and my eyes filled with tears. After giving my hugs and greetings to everyone, we went inside the house where they had prepared *mole*, my favorite meal, to celebrate. Once everyone had left, Yesenia and I were alone together again.

"I missed you," she said, smiling.

"Thank you so much for this," I replied.

"I love you," she said finally, leaning in for a kiss. "Let's put this behind us and move on." With that, she lifted her glass of champagne in the air for cheers. "To the next chapter."

"To the next chapter," I repeated, clinking my glass against hers.

EPILOGUE

"*We can complain because rose bushes have thorns, or rejoice because thorns have roses.*"

—*ALPHONSE KARR*

After going to jail, I realized once again just how blessed my life was and became determined to not make the same mistakes. I thought of Brenda and Boston, hoping they were safe—and that they might get in touch with me once they were free again.

Though it seemed strange that life could return to normal after everything I'd been running from for years, that was what happened. The only difference was that now, I had let go of my secrets and could focus entirely on the present, and what was in front of me.

The subdivision project that Yesenia and I had started with her family years ago finally came to fruition, and after developing and selling lot after lot, the development ended up with a total profit of only $75,000 over three years. While it wasn't much money for all the work that went in, taking on the project in the first place is what had encouraged Yesenia and me to stretch ourselves—and to partner with her family while doing it. Today, we're working on developing 17 acres of riverfront property, a testament to having bigger dreams than ever before.

In the depths of Covid paranoia and fear over what my future would hold, I had written a goal on the chalkboard in my makeshift gym: write a book of everything I'd been through. Though I knew I'd made mistakes that I had to answer for, I wanted a chance to tell my side of the story in full, to explain what led me to do what I did and what lessons I learned. Now, you're holding in your hands the book that I envisioned.

As I finish writing this final chapter, I am looking out at the horizon at a beautiful view of the Caribbean Sea from our rooftop waterfront condo in Holbox, drinking my morning coffee as I salute the rising sun. It is one of 10 rental properties that Yesenia and I have in our portfolio, which includes three waterfront properties we rent out on Airbnb, that give us a passive income of $200,000 a year. It is exactly the amount we determined we would need to retire (or more accurately, to make working optional). We became millionaires as we said we would, and we offered the same option to my mom to retire with our help (though she insisted that she stay busy or else she'd get too restless).

Though I made mistakes and was punished for them, I didn't let them define me or defeat me. I knew my heart and my intentions, and I chose to learn a lesson and move on. I don't suggest anyone imitate my decisions or my path, though I do hope that my choice to keep moving forward in life may inspire others to let go of their own shadows and do the same.

I write all of this not to dwell on money or to brag, but to illustrate a point. It isn't money that buys happiness, because money is just a tool for accomplishing the goals that you visualize and set for yourself. Happiness is the result of your mindset—one that looks at all the complexity and chaos of life, and finds meaning and beauty in it, despite challenges. When you find beauty in everything, you realize that everyone is deeply connected—and as a result, we should be more compassionate, understanding and loving towards one another.

When we find our own sense of growth and harmony in life, we connect to a force that is much more powerful than we are. One that propels us to our dreams. We can tap into that greater power by changing our thoughts and reminding ourselves that the best years of our lives are still to come. While I don't believe that the ego actually ever dies, I do believe that by being aware of its existence, we can separate it from the self, which allows us to be more conscious in recognizing the patterns that appear in our life. By doing so, we can rise above a problem and let it pass beneath us.

There is a victim and there is a warrior inside each of us, and we get to choose which one we want to be. Though there may be some heat and explosions along the way, like alchemists, we too can turn these things into gold, if we are attentive enough in the class of life.

ACKNOWLEDGMENTS

To Yesenia's family, whom I've now adopted as my own, and for the tremendous love and support that they have given me throughout our journey together.

To my Circle of Five—I would not be where I am if it were not for you. Thank you for sharing the secrets of your success and for encouraging others to pursue their dream life!

And to everyone who has crossed my path and has taught me a lesson in life.

ABOUT THE AUTHOR

Carla Moreno is a serial entrepreneur, realtor, real estate investor and author. Born in Guadalajara, Mexico, she has more than five years of experience buying and selling family and luxury real estate. Her online masterclass guides students through wealth creation and spiritual growth. Carla lives in Seattle with her wife and their Tibetan terrier. *Finding the Gold* is her first book.

Made in the USA
Monee, IL
02 November 2023

45705256R00132